# How to Flirt With Women

Discover How to Talk to Women, Never Run Out of
Things to Say & Master the Art of Seduction

By

## Dave Perrotta

# Buyer Bonus

As a way of saying thank you, I'm offering my **"Instant Attraction Toolkit"** that includes three FREE downloads exclusive to my book readers.

**Here's what you'll get:**

1. **"The First Date Playbook"**: A cheat sheet for first date success, with conversation starters, key questions to ask, and tips on creating a memorable experience. That way, you can get her attracted and keep her coming back for more.

2. **"Get a Girlfriend in 30 Days - Audio Guide"**: The exact step-by-step audio guide to meeting, attracting, and dating your dream girl in 30 days or less.

3. **"5 Texting Mistakes that Destroy Attraction - Audio Guide"**: Discover the texting mistakes that turn her off, derail her attraction, and make you look needy. That way, you can smoothly flirt over text, get more dates, and stop losing out on dating opportunities with beautiful women.

**Download your bonuses here:**

**Go to <u>daveperrotta.com/attraction</u> or scan the QR code below:**

# Contents

# Prologue

# The Power of Flirting

# How to Create the "Spark" That Attracts Her

You just got home from an amazing first date. Everything went right. She was beautiful. She laughed at your jokes. The two of you connected. And the entire time, you were thinking, "I could really see myself with this girl!"

You walk back home feeling a sense of giddy, excited energy and can't help but think of the future. Date two, three, and beyond. Settling in at home, you send her a text: "Hey, Emily. I hope you got home safe! Tonight was a lot of fun."

And then?

Crickets.

You don't hear back from Emily until later the next day. But when you read her text, your stomach drops. "Hey, I had fun too! I don't want to waste your time though. I didn't feel a spark, and I don't see this going anywhere. Good luck with everything!"

You put your phone down and let out a sigh. "This is the fourth time something like this has happened in the last couple of months," you explain to your friend. "I'm tired of it, and I don't know what's going wrong!"

Sound familiar?

Maybe you've also had dates where she "didn't feel a spark," or interactions where you thought that all went well but then she ghosted you when you asked to hang out.

Or maybe you've put dating off for a long time and haven't had many opportunities to get out there and meet women who you're excited about.

Whatever the case, there's one missing piece that you need in order to get past these obstacles and attract your ideal kind of woman: the ability to flirt!

**So, what exactly *is* flirting?**

In short, it's the unspoken language of attraction.

It's the sly, back-and-forth subtleties where you don't necessarily come right out and say, "Hey, I'm into you!" Instead, think of it as kind of a secret conversation that goes on below the surface of what's being said.

It's a mix of playful banter, innuendos, teasing looks, and a magnetic vibe that excites both you and the beautiful woman on the other side of the table. It's a fun way of showing interest and expressing romantic intent.

The men who can master this secret language of flirting move through their dating lives with ease. Their conversations flow effortlessly, women chase them, and they hardly ever get that dreaded "I didn't feel a spark" text. In fact, usually they're the ones who have to send that text to the women, as their many dating options have allowed them to have higher standards.

**Why do you need to master it?**

Every truly top-tier man speaks the language of flirting fluently, as do most women.

When you have the ability to flirt, you can connect with ease, make great first impressions, create a "spark" with a woman, and make any interaction or date more fun and memorable.

It's truly an art that grants you admission to the world of women. It allows you to be "the guy" who she giggles over and gets excited about with her friends. And it gives you the ability to strut into any room with confidence, knowing that even the most beautiful woman in the room could be just one conversation or even one look away from giving you her number and setting up a date.

You become a man with confidence, options, and abundance—something most men will never truly experience. These options also allow you to date different women, understand what you like and don't like, and choose a high-quality partner without having to settle.

It also makes for some pretty awesome first dates!

But in contrast, if you never truly master flirting, you'll feel like you're navigating a perpetual solo dance floor, where the music plays but you're standing on the sidelines, unsure of how to join in.

You'll see other guys having success and dating the women they want, and you'll feel left out or like you're "falling behind." You'll miss connections and opportunities with the women you were most excited about and wonder "What could've been."

Overall, you won't be able to fully express yourself to potential mates and life will be less fun.

I know this fate all too well—I've worked with many guys who come from this world where flirting is a foreign language, and I also dealt with it myself for many years before I finally figured things out. But now I can see just how much things can transform once you become fluent.

**Now here's the good news:**

*Any* man can master the art of how to flirt with women.

Whether you're wealthy or struggling financially, naturally charismatic or shy, conventionally attractive or "not naturally good looking," you can absolutely learn this essential skill and apply it in your life.

And in this book, you'll discover exactly how to do just that. You'll no longer have to be on the outside looking in.

It's time to join the party and embrace the adventure that awaits you once you tap into your potential and unleash your true flirting abilities.

But before we dive in, you're likely wondering, "Who is this guy and what does he know about flirting and seduction?" Fair question. I get it. After all, there's a ton of shady characters out there on social media these days preaching questionable advice.

My name is Dave Perrotta, and I've dedicated the last thirteen years of my life to mastering the dating skillset. First (and obviously) for my own sake, and then through coaching thousands of men to do the same.

I started as an insecure guy in my early twenties with no idea how to talk to women or speak the language of flirting. This lack of dating success frustrated me so much that it embedded a deep desire within me to get this part of my life fully handled. And that's exactly what I did, although it took me several years and several thousands of approaches and dates.

But as I transformed my dating life, I saw the rest of my life change, too. Once I could conquer my fear of talking to that cute girl, no fear in my life was off limits. This led me on an epic adventure—I went on to quit my desk job, live in over 20 countries, and start multiple online businesses. And it also inspired me to give back and help other men make the same transformation in *their* dating lives.

You may have seen me on Instagram, TikTok, or YouTube—where I have over 400,000 combined followers—or heard about one of my bestselling books like *Conversation Casanova*.

Over the years, I've worked with men from all walks of life. From 19-year-old guys who've barely ever talked to a girl, 30-somethings who are trying to balance their dating and professional life, and even 60-somethings coming out of decades-long marriages, as well as everyone in between.

I've seen it all. I've come face to face with the mindsets and conversation struggles that hold men back, and I have a deep understanding of how to get you past them. That's what this book is all about. Once you master the art of flirting by following the essential tips and techniques within these pages, your dating life won't be filled with frustration but instead with abundance and fulfillment. You'll have a clear path and plan to attract your ideal partner.

# The 4 Keys to Flirting Like a Pro

This book is divided into four key parts that'll help you master the art of flirting. I suggest reading the chapters in order, as each part will help you understand the next. Then, once you've read the entire book, you can go back and review the material that centers around your biggest sticking points.

### Part 1: Mastering the Flirty Vibe

This section gives you a deeper understanding of flirting.

You'll discover flirting from the woman's perspective so that you'll know what she's attracted to and what signs she'll give off when she likes you. You'll also internalize the key flirting mindsets—without these, every flirting technique will be just a facade. But once you internalize these mindsets, flirting will be a natural part of the way you operate as a man. Then we'll look at some movie examples and breakdowns to help you understand and witness effective flirting in action, along with how to replicate it yourself.

## Part 2: The Flirting Fundamentals

In this section, you'll discover the building blocks of flirting with and meeting attractive women.

We'll cover where to meet them in your everyday life and online, how to get the conversation started, and the actual techniques to flirt with and attract women.

Afterwards, you'll have a toolbox full of great flirting techniques to help you master the art of seduction and never run out of things to say.

## Part 3: How to Flirt in Key Situations

You'll discover exactly how to flirt with women—when you first meet her, when you're on a date or in a group, and when you're texting or messaging on dating apps.

Whatever situation you might come across, you'll know exactly how to break out the flirting techniques, lead things forward, and get her interested.

## Part 4: How to Be a Natural at Flirting

You don't want to have to keep referring back to a book everytime you want to flirt with a girl, right? You want flirting to feel natural—to the point where it feels effortless to charm the ladies like a pro.

That's the point of this section, in which I'll uncover the ten raw skills that'll make you a natural at flirting. These are the exact skills I teach my dating coaching clients—the same skills I used to use myself to effortlessly flirt on the way to meeting my amazing girlfriend. Finally, you'll discover how to easily build these raw flirting skills with a set of small daily habits that'll only take you a few months to master. Once you get these down, your flirting will flow smoothly and effortlessly.

## Remember: Action is King

If you truly want to succeed with flirting and attract the women of your dreams, you've got to take consistent action.

Simply reading books, watching YouTube videos, and listening to podcasts isn't going to cut it. There are no "magic" solutions out there—and this book isn't one either. But if you're ready to take your dating life and flirting abilities seriously, it *will* give you all the tools to succeed. So absorb these words, apply what you learn, and then get ready to embark on an awesome new journey where (unlike so many other guys out there) you'll actually have control over your dating life.

# Part 1

# Mastering the Flirty Vibe

# How Women Flirt

To become great at flirting yourself, you first must understand how *women* flirt. And we've all been there. You're talking to a girl or she catches your eye from across the room, or maybe she just sends you an interesting text, and you think, "Is she flirting with me? Was that laugh platonic…or something more?

When you understand how women flirt, you'll quickly pick up on their cues and be able to tell what's working—as well as what's *not* working.

The nuances of her body language, the tone of her voice, the subtleties of her expressions, and the words she says (and texts) can all let you know exactly where you stand in the interaction. When you're able to read these signals correctly, you'll have effortless conversations without any overthinking and calibrate your advances more smoothly.

Compare this to the average guy, who might as well be a deer in the headlights when attempting to flirt with a woman. He may pick up on her signs some of the time, but that's more luck than skill—and luck isn't repeatable so it won't help you much in the long run. Let's first examine how women flirt in person, and then we'll cover the nuances of how they flirt over text.

## How She Approaches You (Without Saying a Word)

First, you need to understand that women live in a slightly different world than us guys. We can go up and talk to a girl and get rejected, and it's not a big deal. We may *think* that it's a big deal, but no one really bats an eye in the grand scheme of things. We don't actually risk that much, because it's socially acceptable—and even expected—for the man to initiate things. However, from a woman's point of view, approaching a man generally *is* a big deal. If she goes up and gets rejected in front of everyone, it'll feel much harder to live down for her than it is for us. It's not as socially acceptable and so it's more of a social risk. That's why women won't often approach you first—even if you're dressed to the nines with all the "game" in the world and all your fundamentals on point. But women, as crafty as they are, have outsmarted us men. They've figured out a way to approach us without any of the social risk that comes along with getting rejected. They don't need to say a single word, and the men who are "tuned in" know exactly what's going on.

How do they do this? Through something called an "approach invitation." This is where she subtly lets you know that she's interested and gives you an opportunity to come up and talk to her—and then it's on *you* to make your move. And you'd better act fast because if the window closes, you'll likely lose your chance (or another guy may catch on and swoop in). **Below are some of the most common approach invitations women will give you:**

- She'll look at you and smile (even from across the room)

- She'll look in your general direction multiple times for no apparent reason

- She'll position herself nearby you, also for no apparent reason

- She'll pass close by and maybe even brush against you

- She'll ask you an innocent question (if you have any drink recommendations or even for directions)

If she gives you these signs and you like what you see, don't be afraid to move in and go talk to her! But all too often, guys overlook even the most obvious approach invitations. They'll think, "She's probably not looking at me" or "I'm not sure what to say to her anyway," and do nothing. Don't be one of these guys. Instead, just assume that she's attracted to you and then go find out for yourself. I remember one time in Budapest when I was walking through a street of crowded restaurant patios. A beautiful girl caught my eye from about 15 feet away, and I saw her smile. I walked through the restaurant, approached her table, and started a quick conversation. I invited her and her friends to come out with us later that night—they agreed, met us a few hours later, and we had a great time. All from one initial glance from a distance!

These approach invitations are powerful because they allow you to make a "warm approach" (like you already have some familiarity) rather than a "cold approach" (in which the two of you haven't acknowledged each other yet). There's already an expected and assumed level of attraction, especially if you've both made eye contact and smiled. This makes things easier for you.

Now, you won't *always* get these invitations from girls you want to talk to. Often, and especially as you get started on improving, you won't, and so you've got to be prepared to start conversations from scratch. And that's just fine—some of your best conversations will happen this way. I've dated many girls who never gave me an approach invitation at the start.

But just because she hasn't given you an approach invitation doesn't mean she hasn't noticed you—some women just shy away from giving these invitations.

Now you might be wondering, "How do I get more of these approach invitations?"

In short, the better you look and the better you're positioned, the more it will happen. **Here's what you can do to get more women looking your way:**

- Looksmaxx. In other words, optimize your "good looking" potential by improving your style, getting a good haircut, fixing your teeth, building muscle, and having clear skin. When you look good, women will notice.

- Have solid, open posture and a relaxed facial expression. The more laid back and receptive you look, the more inviting you'll appear to women who'd like to meet you.

- Master your positioning. If you see a cute girl in a cafe, sit near her. If you're going for a walk, do so in higher traffic areas where more women can pass by. And if you're out at night, stand in a place where the most women can see you.

## How Women Flirt in Person

Now let's shift to what happens when you're actually talking to a woman. Understanding how she flirts will help you to read women better—as well as become better at flirting yourself.

### Eye Contact

Women can basically speak an entire language with their eyes. They won't just use their eyes to draw you in and get you to approach them but *also* while they're in a conversation with you.

First, you've got the "doggy dinner bowl" eyes. She'll give you this look when she's super into you and eating up everything you say. Her pupils dilate, her eyebrows raise, and her eyes become wide. She wants more and it's very obvious that she's into you. When you get this, it's time to kiss her or take whatever the next step is, like going to a more private location where intimacy might be possible.

Another thing to watch for is prolonged eye contact. When girls aren't interested, they tend to glance away often and avoid giving you their full attention. But when she's fully locked in and staring right into your eyes for most of the conversation, odds are that she's highly interested.

Then you've got the "eye contact, smile, and look down" combo. This can happen when she notices you from across the room, or even in a conversation with you. It often indicates that she's being flirty but also a little shy and bashful.

## What She Says

Women's flirting certainly isn't all non-verbal–they flirt with their words too. It's a good sign if she's doing any of the following:

## Playful Teasing

Maybe she pokes fun at your favorite music or TV show, or even teases you about a story that you shared. Or, while she does this, maybe she gives you a little playful nudge on the arm.

She might even bring up an inside joke about something that came up earlier in the conversation.

This is her way of showing you that she's comfortable enough around you to make jokes and invite you into her world a little bit. Be aware of this and you won't be an "outsider" like the majority of men who "don't get it" when it comes to women.

## Compliments

If she's flirting, she might not be able to resist throwing a compliment or two at you. Maybe she mentions how she loves your smile, the color of your eyes, or even just the fact that you can make her laugh.

All of these are good signs. She's unlikely to compliment guys she's not into, right?

## Innuendos

She might make up her own innuendos or just respond very positively when you weave one into the conversation. Again, this is her way of bringing you "in on the joke" and seeing if you can play ball with some fun banter of your own.

## Testing You

Women's tests are another form of flirting. She might say things like, "Do you say this to every girl?", "You know we're not sleeping together, right?", "Do you really like that kind of music?", and so on.

She's testing to see how you respond and if you're really the guy you make yourself out to be. A lot of guys put on facades, and she wants to make sure that you're not one of them. That's why it's actually a good thing if she tests you—it shows that she wants you to be "that" guy. And if you pass, you're in.

## Future Plans

As she becomes more enamored with you, she might start future-projecting things that the two of you could do together: "I've been wanting to see that show for so long. We should go together!" "So, you like to cook pizza? I'll have to see that for myself!"

She's finding ways to envision spending more time with you.

## Lots of Questions

When she's interested, she'll want to know a lot about you. She might pelt you with questions about your life, interests, and dreams.

She's not just making small talk—she's aiming to get to know the real you.

## Physical Flirting

Women flirt physically, too, through touch and other ways.

She might initiate some of those playful touches mentioned previously after making a joke or teasing you—maybe even a brief hand on the chest while laughing. She's looking to establish a connection and gauge your reaction.

You can initiate this first, too, and see how she reacts. One of my favorite moves on a first date is after leaving the venue and I put my arm around her. If she's warm and leans right into me, I know there's very high interest, and I can give her a quick kiss right then and there as I lead things to the next location.

Then there's physical mirroring, which is a subconscious behavior that indicates rapport and attraction. If she's mimicking your gestures, posture, and movements, she might just be into you.

And perhaps the easiest one to be aware of is proximity. The more she leans into you, the closer she stands, and the more she gets into your "bubble" and allows you into hers, the more she's likely interested. Be aware of her subtle body language cues as well. Is she leaning toward you? Are her feet squarely pointed in your direction while she maintains open posture? These are all great signs.

And one of my favorites to test all this out? Give her a high five during a high point in the conversation. If she clasps your hand with her fingers, there's definite high interest there.

## Following Your Lead

In general, if a woman follows your lead, it means that she likes where things are going.

The two examples above—the high five with the hand clasp and the arm around her with the lean in—exhibit this.

You should always be looking to move things forward as early as you can in the interaction to test her interest level.

For example, if you meet her at the bar, you can move her a few feet over to get out of the way of foot traffic. If you meet her during the day, you can give her a handshake and hold it for a few seconds longer than normal and see if she follows along.

Then, as you get more buy-in and investment from her, you can go for bigger and bigger asks, from a kiss to eventually going back to somewhere more intimate.

## Dressing To Impress

How does she show up to meet you? This is always a tell-tale sign when it comes to first dates.

If she shows up in sweats with a disheveled appearance, she definitely doesn't have much of a stake in the date. But if she comes dressed to impress with heels, a nice dress, her hair done, and flawless makeup, there's zero doubt that she's interested and sees this as a date.

# How Women Flirt Over Text

Now you've got a great understanding of how women flirt in person. But over text? That's a different story, and it's where many guys get confused (and eventually ghosted). They don't know how to pick up on her flirting. Let's solve this below.

## The Extended Word

This has been women's go-to flirting method since texting was invented. A prime example? "Heyyyy"—the more "y"s at the end, the higher her interest level. She also might throw in a "Lmaoooo" or a "Hahahaha," which are other frequent forms of extended phrases.

## Lots of Emojis

As a man, you don't want to overuse emojis—and you *definitely* don't want to use them more than she does. Why? Because it can make you come across a little too eager, needy, or even feminine. But emojis are a woman's bread and butter when it comes to flirting over text, and the more of these she uses, the more it signals that she's into you.

## Voice Messages

I've noticed that this is more of a thing with Latina and Spanish women. They love to send long voice notes in Spanish with a ton of slang (and I have to listen to them ten times so I'm sure of the meaning). Voice notes are becoming a little more common in America too, though. And as you'll learn later in the book, you can use them to your advantage.

Generally, though, she won't take the time to make a voice message unless she's at least somewhat into you, so just the fact that she's sending you one is a good sign.

## Exclamation Points

Women love to spice things up with some extra exclamation points when they're trying to flirt. Just like with the extended word, the more of these she throws in, the more excited she is about talking to you.

## Response Time

A lot of guys get wrapped up in judging a woman's response time in their text conversations. And that's fair enough, because it does matter. If she takes hours (or days) to respond, it means that she's probably got something else tying up her attention—perhaps even another guy. This isn't always the case, and if she's usually down to hang out, you don't need to read too much into it—especially early on.

But if you're several dates in, you've gotten intimate already, and she's *still* taking a long time to respond? There's a good chance that she might not see you as more than a hookup buddy.

Because when she's highly invested and interested in you, her response times should generally either mirror yours or be even quicker.

# What Women Need to Feel Attraction

Simply put, if you don't know what generates attraction in women, they won't try to flirt with you. So let's take a look at a few key factors that generate this attractiveness and make her go wild for you.

## Strong Communication & Flirting Skills

Being able to talk and flirt confidently is a must in the dating world. You can max out your potential in every other area and make yourself into a "great package," but if you can't communicate and flirt, it won't matter. You won't be able to market yourself or make her feel positive emotions.

This is why there are so many men who are successful with their careers and finances but can't attract or hold down a quality woman.

This is also why a guy like me, when I was in my early twenties and completely broke, had much more dating success than the doctors, lawyers, and other wealthier guys I hung out with.

Once you've mastered flirting, everything else becomes much easier.

## Capability & Competence

Women love a man who's capable, competent, and can handle anything that's thrown his way.

They toss a verbal jab or a test at him? He can pass it no problem.

An issue comes up in his business? He can figure it out.

Whether it's excelling in your career or mastering a hobby, showing competence signals to a woman that you're dependable and can provide stability in a relationship. It's also just plain sexy for her to see you do something really well, like mastering the intricacies of a fun and flirty conversation.

## Confidence

Hey, I know that you don't need to read a book on flirting to understand that women love confidence, but it's still important to point out!

Confidence is like a magnet that draws women in. It's about knowing who you are and what you bring to the table without coming across as arrogant. When you have confidence, it shows that you're comfortable in your own skin and not afraid to go after what you want. It's that inner strength and self-assurance that make a man irresistible to women.

What's interesting is that the more capable and competent you become, the more confident you become as well. It comes with repetition, so get those reps in!

## Warmth

You want there to be an element of warmth to your personality and flirting. Women *love* this. It makes them feel that you're "in this together" and that you're different from other guys. It makes them feel like the two of you are on the same team.

**To give off a sense of warmth, you need a mix of the following:**

- **Authenticity:** This comes down to being self-amused and approaching interactions with genuine interest, sincerity, and openness.

- **Empathy:** This is the ability to understand and share her feelings. It shows you're attuned to her emotions and fosters a sense of connection.

- **Kindness:** This could be a simple gesture like opening the car door for her, handling the bill on a date, or walking her home.

- **Approachability:** It's all about having an open and friendly demeanor that makes others feel comfortable in your presence.

- **Positive Energy:** This is a mix of having a sense of hopefulness in the future and intentionally putting yourself in a positive mental state.

- **Good Intentions:** You need to have genuinely good intentions for every woman you meet. No bitterness—just the willingness to have a good experience and add some sort of value rather than extract it.

Essentially, when you have warmth, she can feel that you genuinely want the best for her. She knows that you're not going to do anything creepy or weird and that she can have a good level of trust in you.

The more of this she feels, the more she'll open up and want to go on adventures with you. It also gives her the freedom to show you her "secret side"—the side of her that nobody else really ever gets to see. This is when her walls completely go down, and it's a beautiful thing. You get the privilege of experiencing her in her genuine, most authentic form, which lays the groundwork for an incredibly deep connection.

When you really have this dialed in, women can show you more in a single interaction than they've shown to serious boyfriends they've had in the past. You'll hear a lot of, "I've never said this to anyone before" and "I feel like I can be myself around you." And she won't be saying these things in a platonic way, either.

## Self-Awareness

There are a lot of people out there who basically go through their entire lives as drones. They live an unexamined existence and never really know themselves. Remember that your level of self-awareness becomes apparent very quickly in your interactions with women.

Women are attracted to men who know themselves well—men who reflect on their actions but also their inner thoughts, feelings, and motivations.

**Here's how to be more self-aware:**

- **Practice Mindfulness:** Try things like meditation, deep breathing exercises, or simply taking a few moments each day to pause and check in with yourself.

- **Reflect on Your Values and Beliefs:** What matters most to you and why? Aligning your actions with your values can help you live a more authentic life.

- **Seek Feedback:** Ask trusted friends, family members, or mentors for honest feedback about your strengths and areas for improvement. Be open to that feedback (even if it ruffles your feathers a bit) and use it as an opportunity for growth.

- **Journaling:** Keep a journal to document your thoughts, emotions, and experiences. Writing can be a powerful tool for self-reflection and self-discovery, even if you just jot out some thoughts for five to ten minutes at the beginning or end of your day.

Above all, you need to realize that nobody has it all figured out—and that you're no exception to the rule. Always be open to learning, getting better, and taking in feedback.

Now, if we step back and look at each of these five traits we've just examined, we can see that they'll help you show women a good time in the moment but also give them confidence in your long-term potential. Developing these qualities gives you a big edge over other guys in the dating marketplace, and it allows you to have much more control over your dating life.

## Key Takeaways

- **Awareness:** You now understand the woman's perspective on things, as well as how she actively and subconsciously flirts with you. This will make it obvious if your flirting attempts are working (or falling flat).

- **Approach Invitations:** Be aware of these, as they're her way of approaching you without actually doing so. When you get an invitation, move in fast before the window closes.

- **Body Language and Verbal Cues:** Pay attention to the signals she's giving—this will give you a good read on where the interaction is currently at and how quickly you may be able to move things to the next step.

- **Be Aware of Her Texting:** Extended words, lots of emojis and exclamation points, and fast response times convey interest and excitement.

- **Up Your Game:** Build out the traits and qualities that attract women—strong communication and flirting skills, competence and capability, confidence, warmth, and self-awareness.

# The 5 Flirty Mindsets That Make You Irresistible

Good flirting starts in the mind. Flirty, sexy men think differently than the average guy. You might even say that they have a unique approach to life and a fresh perspective on dating and women.

Plus, the right mindset can transform flirting from a nerve-wracking experience into a confident and enjoyable interaction.

Let's examine the five most important flirting mindsets that'll make you stand out among all the other guys and become irresistible to women.

## 1. The World Is My Playground

Picture a guy who approaches dating with a rigid and serious mindset. He sees every interaction with a woman as a test of his worthiness and whether or not he's truly "good enough." He constantly worries about screwing up and feels like he needs to perform at the top of his game at all times. In short, rejection terrifies him.

He doesn't see the world as a playground—he sees it as a battlefield. He's so hyperfocused on his own insecurities and shortcomings that he can't just let go and have fun. And he wouldn't *dream* of showing vulnerability or taking unnecessary social risks, as this might make him seem weak and inadequate.

Do you see the problem here? He's so concerned about how he looks and whether he's good enough that he comes across as stiff and insecure around women. And this is a *major* turnoff. As a result, his attempts at flirting feel contrived and fall flat.

This is how many men approach flirting, as well as life in general. And it's no surprise—they spend most of their days with this mindset, approaching their career or job like a battlefield. It's hard to adjust when it comes to interacting with women.

But let me offer a contrast to this.

Imagine yourself as a kid again, stepping foot onto the playground. You look around and see the other kids playing, the jungle gym waiting to be explored, and the sand begging for you to dash around and play tag in it. You've got a sense of wonder and excitement, and the possibilities feel endless.

Now, translate that same mindset into your interactions with women.

Instead of taking yourself so seriously and viewing dating as a high-stakes game in which every move is scrutinized and judged, see it as an opportunity for fun and enjoyment.

You can approach that girl, say that innuendo, and make that joke—you might not know what'll happen but at least it'll be interesting.

Embrace the spontaneity and unpredictability of human connection, just like you'd embrace the twists and turns of a jungle gym or a fun game of tag with your childhood friends.

When you see the world as your playground, flirting becomes effortless and natural. You're not afraid to take risks or make mistakes because, hey—it's all part of the game. You can tease and banter with ease, knowing that it's all in good fun. And if things *don't* go as planned, you simply brush it off and move on to the next adventure.

With this mindset, you can also approach women with genuine curiosity and interest. You no longer view them as potential conquests or obstacles to overcome—instead, you view them as fellow players in the game of life. You're genuinely interested in getting to know them, not just as potential romantic partners but as people with their own fun and unique experiences and stories.

We can take this one step further by looking at it this way: Every time you leave your front door, there's an adventure to be had.

That woman walking by on the sidewalk, the cute cashier at the grocery store, the pretty girl who glances over to you at the gym—any one of them could be your next fun conversation or, who knows, maybe even your next girlfriend. When you have an openness to life rather than that rigid "I'm going about my day and I don't have time to notice or talk to women" mentality, the possibilities become endless.

So be the guy on the playground and embrace your inner childlike wonder. It's all a game anyway, so you might as well get in there and play it and have a little fun!

## 2. Rejection Is a Win

The men who are best at flirting are able to separate rejection from their own personal self-worth. They understand that not every interaction or date will lead to a positive outcome, and they're okay with that. Instead, they see rejection as an opportunity for growth and self-improvement.

Maybe they talk to a girl, make a joke that falls flat, and realize that they need to be a little more socially calibrated and attentive to social cues. Perhaps they discover that they're not as compatible with certain types of women as they initially thought. This allows them to more quickly filter for women who might actually be a good fit.

After coaching thousands of guys, I can confidently say that the men with this mindset improve astronomically faster than those who get bent out of shape and dwell on every single rejection. Instead of needing to jump a giant mental hurdle of angst and frustration every time a woman ghosts them or brushes off their attempt at a second date, they let it roll right off their shoulders and keep moving along.

This courage in the face of rejection also makes their flirting more smooth. Again, they don't fear risk taking, and so they come off as more fun and with more of an edge than most other guys, which ultimately makes them stand out.

And if you think about it, rejection is actually a *win*. The woman who turned you down saved you time. Instead of having to pine over someone who's uninterested, you have the freedom to move on and meet women who *are* interested, and that's the whole point.

## 3. I Love Women

A man who's good at flirting must genuinely love women—the two go hand-in-hand. And quite honestly, that's what a lot of these red pill guys don't seem to understand.

A man who genuinely loves women sees them as complex and fascinating instead of prizes to be won. There's a genuine kindness behind everything he does and says, without any kind of ulterior motive or agenda. For him, flirting isn't about manipulating women. It's about being in the moment, enjoying one another's presence, being self-amused, and engaging in the subtle dance of attraction that comes with flirting. He wants to get to know her on a deeper level, have some fun banter, and share unique moments together.

That split second in time when you're locked in with a beautiful woman, totally on the same wavelength, and knowing that you just "get each other"—it's one of the most magical moments this life has to offer.

With these kinds of interactions, there's a big difference between the warm sincerity that comes from a man who loves women compared to the insincere crassness from a man who's bitter about them.

# 4. I Am in the Moment

Imagine a man who approaches interactions with women with a laser focus on the present. He's fully engaged, attentive, and invested in the conversation, making the woman feel like she's the only thing that matters at that point in time.

He puts aside any distractions and worries, as well as his thoughts about the future or the past. He's even able to put aside what this girl might be thinking of him. His entire focus is on her words, expressions, and body language—everything that encompasses the present interaction.

He doesn't simply wait until it's his turn to speak; he listens intently, asks genuine questions, makes playful teases, and shows authentic curiosity. This allows him to pick up on the subtle nuances in her moods, emotions, and reactions in real-time. This full presence helps him create a sense of intimacy that goes beyond the surface-level small talk she has with every other guy.

She feels like she's experiencing something special and unique with him. It's a memorable encounter, and she wants more.

If you're looking for some sort of a "secret sauce" to flirting, this is it. Every guy who's a natural with women has this down pat. Things are able to flow smoothly and he's fully engaged. Remember—this is a stark contrast for women, who are used to dealing with neurotic, overly analytical men.

We'll examine more about how to be present later in this book. But here's an easy tip: When you talk to a beautiful woman, enjoy it! It's supposed to be fun, not some complicated jigsaw puzzle you struggle to figure out. The relaxed and laid-back presence you embody will easily make you stand out.

# 5. Acceptance

You've got to be okay with that fact that not every interaction will spark fireworks.

There'll be women with whom you have amazing chemistry with, and over the span of a quick conversation, you'll feel like you've known her for years and you completely click. It's beautiful when this happens but, sadly, it just isn't the case each and every time.

That's because there are levels to chemistry and connection. Some girls you'll click with on an okay level, and this can be sufficient for a casual hookup sort of situation. Then there'll be others where it feels like the connection is a 10/10, and these are your serious relationship potential girls. You still need to test if there's compatibility, but compatibility doesn't matter if there's no chemistry.

But there'll also be times when you do everything right, and for whatever reason, there's just no chemistry there. The conversation feels forced. Maybe she's having a bad day, or maybe your personalities are just completely incompatible.

Think of it this way: Not every person you meet is going to be your new best friend, right? The same goes for romantic connections. You won't click with every girl you flirt with, and that's totally fine.

When you accept this reality, it takes the pressure off. You can relax and enjoy the process without worrying about every interaction needing to lead somewhere. And you know what? It's actually liberating.

Because when you're not desperately trying to force a connection, you come across as more genuine and confident. And that's attractive in itself.

So the next time you're flirting with a girl and things don't quite click, just shrug it off. It's no big deal—there are plenty of more opportunities out there. Just keep improving your flirting fundamentals and confidence, put yourself out there, and you'll meet girls you *do* click with. That's the goal after all, right?

## Key Takeaways

- **Embrace Playfulness:** Approach interactions with women with the mindset that the world is your playground. Let go of rigid expectations and see each conversation as an opportunity for fun, enjoyment, and adventure.

- **See Rejection as a Win:** Instead of fearing rejection, regard it as a chance to learn something new, as well as to grow and improve. Rejection allows you to refine your flirting skills and filter for women who are genuinely interested.

- **Cultivate a Genuine Love for Women:** Cut out all the red pill mindsets and develop a sincere love and respect for women. This will help you flirt from a place of warmth, kindness, and good intentions.

- **Be Present:** Be fully there when you interact with women. Listen attentively, ask genuine questions, and show interest in what they're saying.

- **Embrace Acceptance:** You won't click with every girl you meet, and that's totally fine. At the same time, there'll be levels to the chemistry and connection with girls that you do click with.

# Flirt Like James Bond: Movie Character Examples to Build Your Flirting Style

If you've never been great at flirting, nor have had any friends who've really mastered it, it can be a challenge to understand what good flirting actually looks like.

But thanks to Hollywood, you don't have to imagine it all on your own. There are a few movie characters who are flirting masters, and there are hard-hitting lessons you can learn from each one and apply to your own flirting methods.

If you haven't seen these movies, it'd be a good idea to check them out—or at least watch a few clips of them on YouTube. **We'll examine three specific characters:**

- James Bond from the classic spy movies

- Dex from The Tao of Steve

- Jacob Palmer from Crazy, Stupid, Love

## The Smooth Moves of James Bond

Whenever a coaching client of mine is having a freak out or going into full panic mode about women, I like to reference James Bond.

Bond's got confidence in spades, and he's unfazed even by the most intense of situations. Whether he's facing down a villain or wooing a femme fatale, he never breaks a sweat.

He's also got a knack for witty banter. As is clear in every interaction, he's got a comeback for everything and he can pass any test that women throw his way. Now, bear in mind that you don't need to be a crime-fighting, world-renowned, undercover spy to exhibit these abilities yourself, as we'll see below.

Let's look at a few techniques you can use in your flirting, perfectly demonstrated by Bond.

## 1. Observation & Adaptability

Remember when we examined how presence is key in your interactions? Bond has this down pat.

He's always attuned to social cues and signals given off by those around him. This allows him to adapt his flirting style to suit the preferences and personality of the woman he's interacting with.

**Let's take his encounter with Sévérine in Skyfall as an example (you can check out the clip here:** https://bit.ly/skyfall-flirting**).**

Bond saunters into the casino and locks eyes with her, and she meets his gaze with a mix of apprehension and curiosity. "Now you can afford to buy me a drink," she starts, noticing his winnings.

Bond pauses, looks into her eyes, and says, "Maybe I'll even stretch to two."

Right from the start, their conversation is laced with innuendo and subtle hints of danger. Sévérine, initially guarded, finds herself drawn to Bond's magnetic charisma.

At one point, she's about to leave but Bond gently grabs her forearm and makes an observation. He mentions her tattoo and then calls out her feeling of vulnerability. By doing so, he creates a sense of intimacy between them and lays the groundwork for a stronger connection—as well as more banter and flirting.

This interaction gives a perfect example of passing a woman's test. Instead of getting flustered when she says, "Now you can afford to buy me a drink," Bond stays cool, calm and collected. He simply agrees and exaggerates a little bit, saying that maybe he can buy her two, and then keeps going unfazed. You can use this in your own interactions.

**For example**, if a woman says, "You know we're not sleeping together, right?", you could agree and exaggerate with a sly smile before saying, "Of course not. You've got to wine and dine me first!"

## 2. Leading & Seizing the Moment

**Let's look at Bond's encounter with Solange in Casino Royale (you can see the clip here:** https://bit.ly/Royale-flirting**).**

After his high-stakes poker game with an adversary named Dimitrios, Bond wins Dimitrios' Aston Martin. He goes to pick the car up from the valet when Dimitrios wife approaches, not realizing that her husband has lost the car in the bet.

As she sees Bond getting into the car, she recognizes her mistake.

**Solange:** "No wonder he was in such a foul mood. My mistake."

**Bond:** "Can I give you a lift home?"

**Solange:** "That would really send him over the edge…I'm afraid I'm not that cruel."

**Bond:** "Or perhaps you're just out of practice."

**Solange:** (laughing) "Perhaps."

**Bond:** "What about a drink at my place?"

**Solange:** "You have a place? Is it close?"

**Bond:** "Very."

They share an interested stare for a few moments.

**Solange:** "One drink."

And just like that, a night of adventure and passion begins.

There's a few things that happen here:

First, Bond recognizes the opportunity. He senses that she has a mix of curiosity and attraction, and he seizes the moment to push things further.

This isn't to say that you should be attempting this with married women (yikes!), but it demonstrates that it's key to be attuned to her state and how she's feeling.

She attempts to dismiss him from the start by saying she's not that cruel, and then she begins walking away. This is where most men would give up and let it go, thinking that it's over. Or they'd plead for her to reconsider. But Bond knows better.

When he drops the line, "Or perhaps you're just out of practice," he passes her test and reels her back in.

Recognizing the opportunity, he goes in for the close by asking if she wants a drink at his place. From there, it's clear that it's "on."

This shows just how key it is to go in for the close when you have the window of opportunity. Had Bond hesitated or second guessed himself, the window would've closed and he would've missed his chance.

I learned very early on that when you have the opportunity, you've got to take it and act decisively. If you can do this confidently and there's attraction there already, women will usually follow your lead.

And finally, with both this and the first example, Bond exhibits the importance of staying observant and responsive to a woman's signals, as well as understanding when to push things slightly while still respecting her boundaries and comfort level. This keeps the interaction exciting and makes it easier to gently guide things forward.

# The Laid-Back Allure of Dex from The Tao Of Steve

Based on appearances, Dex may seem like the polar opposite of James Bond. He's no international spy—he's a part-time kindergarten teacher. But he's got a similar essence of the laid-back cool and confidence of James Bond.

He draws his flirting "game" from the Tao Te Ching and iconic figures like Steve McQueen. **His philosophy revolves around three principles:**

**1. Be Desireless:** This is all about being nonchalant and indifferent to the outcomes of your interactions with women. Instead of trying too hard to impress or seeking validation, he exudes an aura of self-assuredness and detachment.

**2. Be Excellent:** His second principal shows the importance of personal excellence and self-improvement. He doesn't need to brag, but he might casually mention a cool project he's working on or a captivating story from his travels, demonstrating his passion and ambition.

**3. Be Gone:** This is all about knowing when to exit gracefully. He understands that lingering too long or being too clingy can ruin the allure. He gets that it's better to leave the woman wanting more.

This is surprisingly sound dating advice from a Hollywood movie. Being detached from the outcome, pushing toward personal excellence, leaving her wanting more, and avoiding neediness are all common traits of men who succeed with women.

**A great example comes early on in the movie when Dex flirts with the bartender at a party (clip here:** https://bit.ly/tao-of-steve-flirting).

When ordering a drink, Dex discovers that she's a college student studying philosophy and religion—and also that she doesn't know how to make a Long Island iced tea.

He starts by showing genuine interest in her field of study and then asks a few thought-provoking questions about her philosophical views, listening attentively to her responses. Then, to keep the mood light and fun, he shifts toward playful banter and teases her in a friendly way, showing her how to make a Long Island iced tea through the lens of philosophy and religion.

"A Long Island iced tea is like a survey course in world religions. We're starting with the Far East—you've got Hinduism, Taosim… (as he pours Vodka and then names a few more) …you've got zoroastrianism… Did you know that Zoroastrians considered dogs the equal of men?"

"I know I do," the bartender replies.

"Good answer," Dex says.

This is where most guys usually go off the rails. They get on a serious subject early on and stick with it, never adding any fun to the interaction. It's a nice conversation, but nothing more than that, and it stays platonic. You need to engage more than her intellectual side if you want to attract her.

But Dex isn't done yet. The bartender is clearly engaged through all of this, and when Dex finishes, she laughs and asks, "So, uh, does this type of thing usually work on young philosophy students?"

Again, most guys would crash and burn here and say something like, "Oh, no—I didn't mean it like that!" or "Sorry I wasn't trying to offend you!"

Instead, Dex stays cool and adds the cherry on top of a quick flirting masterclass: "I don't know. Did it work on you?"

She laughs, and Dex perfectly passes the test.

## The Charm of Jacob in Crazy, Stupid, Love

In this movie, Jacob (played by Ryan Gosling) is the epitome of the confident and suave ladies' man.

He's got the look—his style is on point, he's in shape, and totally looksmaxxed—and he's also got the communication skills to back it up.

He hits the same bar throughout the movie and effortlessly picks up women by using his famous line, "You wanna get out of here?" to bring them back to his place.

But the most iconic scene—and also the one from which you can learn the most about flirting with and approaching women—is when he attempts to pick up

**Hannah (played by Emma Stone; have a look at the clip here:** https://bit.ly/Gosling-flirting).

Jacob struts up to Hannah and her friend mid-conversation, and he breaks in with an observational opener. They're talking about Conan O'Brien and how they think he looks like a carrot.

"Who looks like a carrot?"

This is a perfect observational opener. It assumes familiarity, as it allows him to seamlessly transition into the conversation. It also engages both Hannah and her friend, and he keeps them engaged and acknowledges them both throughout the conversation.

This is a key thing guys screw up when flirting and talking to groups of women. They only talk to the girl they're interested in and ignore the rest of the group. Eventually, the other girls in the group get annoyed and drag their friend away. But because Jacob keeps the friend engaged, she's on his side the whole time.

"We're talking about Conan O'Brien," Hannah's friend replies. "My friend Hannah here thinks he's sexy."

"That's weird, because I think your friend Hannah here is really sexy," Jacob replies.

It's forward, but it comes across as very confident. "Oh my God—you did *not* just say that," Hannah replies, jokingly surprised. There's the first test.

"What are you, a lawyer?" he quips back. There's a quick pattern interrupt—he doesn't answer her question literally and appears unfazed.

And as it turns out, she *is* studying to be a lawyer.

"Aren't you a little old to be using cheesy pick-up lines?" Hannah replies.

"Objection, Your Honor. Leading the witness," Jacob says, playing up on her law background.

Then he breaks into a quick roleplay, as he pretends to be the defense attorney and Hannah is the judge. This allows them to let loose and have fun with each other, and the courtroom setting provides a structured framework for their banter.

He does stumble a little bit unnecessarily from here, saying that he noticed her a couple of hours earlier and thinks that she's beautiful. This isn't needed for where he is in the interaction. Then he tries to push it further while she's testing him—when he hasn't fully passed the tests—which is a bad idea. And asking if she finds him attractive comes across a tad needy; I wouldn't recommend doing that in your interactions.

But then he gets back on track with the courtroom roleplay and saves it a bit. He tells a good story about seizing the day and living in the moment, which is great—you want a woman feeling adventurous around you, as she'll be more apt to go on adventures with you. But this is the wrong context to do it in. If you're going to attempt this, it should be framed as a story that naturally comes up in conversation rather than as an argument trying to convince her to be adventurous. He also comes off a tad too pushy by repeatedly asking her for a drink when she's given him very little buy-in up to that point.

It ends with Hannah rejecting him, at least this time, but he's laid a solid enough foundation and created a memorable experience in her mind. She'll return later and he eventually *does* take that next step with her.

So, there are some good and bad things there—both wise to be aware of. And it's worth noting, too, that not every interaction you have will be perfect. You'll make mistakes, and if your communication fundamentals are on point, women will often be forgiving. But if you make too many in a row or in a short period of time, it can blow up in your face. You want that perfect balance of assuredness and awareness.

## Key Takeaways

- **Observation and Adaptability:** James Bond's ability to observe social cues and adapt his flirting style accordingly is a crucial lesson. Being attuned to her signals allows for a more dynamic and engaging interaction, and it allows you to tweak your flirting style to match her personality.

- **Seize the Moment:** Bond's readiness to recognize opportunities and take decisive action highlights why confidence and initiative are key in flirting. Waiting for the perfect moment may mean missing out on potential connections, and once the attraction window closes, it's over. If you don't act fast, you risk missing your chance.

- **Playful Banter and Wit:** Dex from The Tao of Steve and Jacob from Crazy, Stupid, Love showcase the power of witty banter while flirting. Keeping the conversation light-hearted and fun can create a strong rapport and make interactions more memorable.

- **Balance Confidence with Respect:** Confidence is key, but it's also important to be aware of and respect her boundaries. James

Bond's assertiveness is tempered with respect for Solange's comfort level, and he guides things forward according to that measure.

# Part 2

# The Flirting Fundamentals

# Where To Meet Women

At this point, you've got a deeper understanding of how to flirt, and we'll continue building on that throughout the rest of the book. But before you can use these skills, you (of course) need to know where to meet women!

Lots of guys struggle with this, especially in the years since COVID—more people are working from home and getting out of the house less on a day-to-day basis.

But with a little intention and an open mind, it's surprisingly easy to meet women in your daily routine, as well as on a casual night out.

And keep in mind that the point isn't to pigeonhole yourself into just one of these ways. You might crush it with online dating, but then things dry up for a few weeks or a month. If you can't approach women in person, you'll be stuck.

But if you've got the power to meet women anywhere, any time, and with any method, your well will never run dry. You'll have plenty of opportunities to create dating abundance so that you can find the right partner.

In this chapter, we'll examine where to meet women during the day, at night, and online.

# During the Day

Remember—every time you leave your door, you should see it as an adventure. When you have this mindset, you'll have the openness needed to seize opportunities when they come your way.

## Gyms & Fitness Classes

"You can't approach a girl at the gym, bro! She's busy working out!" A TikTok video of mine went viral a few years ago to the tune of millions of views, and it was about how to approach women at the gym.

I had no idea how controversial this subject was, for both men *and* women. Some are vehemently against it while some others are totally for it.

But everything I teach, coach, and talk about is based on experience, not theory. This is something I've tested myself, as well as with thousands of clients over the years. And from that experience, I can say that women are totally open to being talked to at the gym if you do it right (and, of course, respectfully).

Also, it's great for meeting quality women who take care of themselves and have similar values—after all, if you meet at the gym, you're both into self-care and working out.

**The keys to talking to women respectfully at the gym:**

- Only approach women when they're between sets or entering/leaving the gym.

- Have one or two casual conversations over a week or two before you ask her out so that you can gauge her interest. If she doesn't seem engaged, don't bother asking her out—just keep it friendly.

- Talk to guys at the gym, too. It's a great place to make male friends, and you also won't seem like "that guy" who only talks to all the women.

When it comes to workout classes like yoga, you can have some quick casual conversations before and after class.

## Grocery Stores

These are perfect spots for meeting women. Grocery stores are casual environments where people have their guard down and it's easy to strike up conversations. Plus, there's plenty of conversation fodder—there's something new for every aisle, and you can also tease her about what's in her shopping cart. There's really no lack of observational conversation starters.

**For example**, let's say that you're standing by the avocados. You could ask, "Hey, do you know how to find the perfect ripe avocado? I can never tell if it's just right!"

Another bonus when it comes to grocery stores is that usually people aren't in a rush there, and so it's a relaxed environment where women will generally have a little bit of time to talk.

## Parks

This applies to both dog parks and regular parks.

In a regular park, you might find women casually strolling through or even perched up somewhere with a book in hand or with headphones in.

These are all perfect opportunities to start a conversation. If she's wearing headphones, you can ask for playlist recommendations. If she's reading a book, you can make a comment about that. Easy stuff.

**Here's a viral video of me approaching a girl at a park in Berlin, Germany: (**https://bit.ly/park-approach**)**

it'll give you a little extra context and motivation to approach the next girl you see in your own park!

And as far as dog parks go, you can make a comment or ask a question about her dog to get the conversation started. Or, if you get lucky, maybe your dog goes and plays with her dog and does some of the leg work for you!

## The Mall

Malls in America aren't as good as they used to be for meeting women, but they're still okay choices with plenty of foot traffic going through them. You'll definitely have at least some opportunities.

Malls outside of the USA, however, like in Latin America or Asia, are bustling more than ever before. It seems like a new mall pops up every month in Bangkok, and somehow, it's always crowded. So, if you're living in (or visiting!) a place where mall culture is still huge, definitely take advantage.

Otherwise, you can simply add malls to your toolbox and break them out when some of these other places aren't available, like perhaps in the winter time.

## Busy Downtown Areas

If you live in a big city, you'll want to frequent its bustling urban centers. Peak hours are typically weekend afternoons and early evenings, and also weekday early evenings when everyone gets out of work.

This is where I earned my stripes in the early days of my dating journey, as I met many women near Boylston and Newberry streets in downtown Boston.

These types of areas have high foot traffic, though you'll tend to see more women in a rush than in some of the other locations. That's because they're all usually making their way to and from work, so be cognizant of that. Aim to talk to girls that don't look like they're speeding down the sidewalk.

## Boardwalks & The Beach

If you can swing it, these are some of my favorite places to meet women. Of course, not every city or state offers them, but take advantage if they're available to you.

Boardwalks and beaches offer a super relaxed atmosphere and a scenic view, and people are a lot more chilled out than they might be in a downtown type of setting. Plus, women at the beach and on the boardwalk typically have some time on their hands, and it can be an easy place for an "instant date" where you can transition an initial conversation to a full-on date right then and there.

This was one of my favorite things about living in Playa Del Carmen, Mexico. It has a boardwalk type of atmosphere (called La Quinta) right alongside a beautiful beach.

My logistics were set up well—I lived only one street away from the beach. This made it easy to approach girls there, and I had a place to take them back to if things escalated to the next level.

The other nice part about the beach is that women are often on vacation and feeling a tad more adventurous. When she's got a carpe diem attitude, she tends to be open to getting intimate a little more quickly if that's what you're looking to do.

## Coffee Shops & Lunch Spots

This is perfect for you guys who work from home. Instead of working from your house every single day, take your laptop to a coffee shop with a great vibe. Sit down in the vicinity of a cute girl and ask her for the WiFi password or what she recommends on the menu. You've already got a few easy conversation starters built into the place. And if your job doesn't allow you to work from home, you can pop into coffee shops in your free time or just go out and grab lunch somewhere cool and popular.

Back when I lived in Bogota, I often met up with my friend at a salad spot for a quick bite to eat in between work sessions.

On one occasion, we saw a group of two cute Colombian women in the corner enjoying a meal. My friend went up and talked to them first, and then I joined in a minute later. They were happy to talk to us, and I ended up taking my girl out on several dates and enjoying a great time with her around Colombia. And all it took was a quick, two-minute conversation with her before I returned to the table to eat with my friend. Don't let opportunities like these slip!

## The Farmer's Market

When it comes to meeting women, farmer's markets are like grocery stores on steroids. You've got all the good things about grocery stores but mixed with an open-air environment, more of a chill atmosphere, and even more health-focused women.

If you've got one of these in your area, you should definitely check it out. And it's an easy opportunity to see if she has similar eating habits and values, too.

**For example**, I like to eat a lot of meat, so I know if she's at the grass-fed meat stand or lined up at the raw milk dairy stand, we'll probably get along well!

## Bookstores & Libraries

It's hard to believe sometimes, but bookstores and libraries are still alive and kicking. They may not be as popular as in decades past, but you can absolutely still meet women there.

These places offer a quiet and comfortable environment, easy for starting a conversation in. They're usually not too crowded either, and so you don't need to worry about too many people eavesdropping on your conversation. Plus, there's lots of conversation fodder here—everything from the book aisle she's in to the book she's reading.

# At Night

"I'm not a partier, man. I don't like to meet women at night." "There are no quality girls out at night!"

"No, I don't drink, so I can't go out."

I've heard these things *a million* times. And I get it—nightlife has a reputation for lower-quality women and a lot of drinking.

But to be honest, these aren't good excuses to completely avoid these environments.

First, who says that you need to drink when you go out? You can have plenty of fun sober. Second, you don't need to go to a huge techno club every time you go out. You can go to more chill places—places where there's actually a higher volume of quality women.

And, again, I say this based on my experience from coaching many guys in different environments, as well as meeting my own girlfriends in different ways—during the day, at night, and online (which we'll get to in a bit).

What's unique about nightlife is that it gives you the highest volume of attractive women in a small vicinity. You can't get that anywhere else, not even in really high foot-traffic places. Even if only for getting tons of practice in a short amount of time, it's worth exploring what some nightlife has to offer.

Now as far as where to go, let's look at some options.

## Upscale Bars & Lounges

These are far and away my go-to choice when it comes to nightlife. This is where you'll find high-quality, classy women, and the music isn't blaring so it's easy to start and maintain a conversation.

Most women who go to these environments are open to chatting—and they're usually in smaller groups which makes it even easier to approach them. Plus, people aren't usually getting plastered drunk like they typically do at big clubs, and there's less stimulation. It's easy to get a woman's attention squarely focused on you at these places.

If you can find it, the perfect mix is an upscale lounge that has a small dance floor or dance room. This allows you to get the best of both worlds.

## Other Nightlife

### Dive Bars

These are more cozy, unpretentious kinds of venues. They're certainly not high end, but they offer relaxing atmospheres where it's very easy to get conversations going.

I recommend checking these out during the week. You can pop in and get a game of billiards going with friends, and if you see a cute girl, you can go say hi.

### Concerts & Live Music Venues/Music Festivals

These atmospheres aren't the most ideal for making long-term connections. Most people go in big groups, there's a lot of stimulation, and if you hit it off with a girl, you can't easily leave to somewhere more intimate, at least not for a few hours until the show is over.

However, they can be great for chatting up a bunch of people, making new friends, and getting some practice in. These are more for the experience of having fun, and any girls you meet along the way are a nice bonus.

### Big Nightclubs

These also have a lot of stimulation and lots of big groups. That said, you can get plenty of conversations going, and you can bring girls to the dance floor as well, which makes it a little easier to escalate things.

Big nightclubs present more of a fast-paced game, though. You've got to be well-versed in the flirting techniques we'll dive into, especially push-pull and leading/dominance—otherwise you won't be able to keep women engaged over the course of the night.

*How to Flirt with Women*

# Online

Meeting women online used to be fairly taboo about 15 years ago, but times have definitely changed. These days, if you're not meeting women online, you're playing the game with a serious handicap. Later on, we'll dive into how to flirt online, but for now let's take a look at the best ways to get started on bringing your internet dating game well up to par.

## The Best Dating Apps

This depends a bit on where you're located. If you're in Europe or Latin America,

**For example**, Tinder and Bumble are the most popular dating apps, but Hinge is gaining traction.

In the USA, Hinge is one of the more premium dating apps, while Bumble is decently second-tier, and Tinder tends to be the most spammy, catering to a younger crowd and filled with plenty of bots and fake profiles.

**Here's a quick look at each of the most popular dating apps:**

- **Hinge** brands itself as more of a relationship-focused app, and the women on there tend to be looking for relationships more than anything else (although plenty are open to short-term flings). As I mentioned, it's one of the more premium dating apps—and it's also my #1 choice for the USA.

- **Bumble** is the go-to in Latin America but also widely used throughout the USA and Europe. The unique spin with Bumble is that only women can start the conversation after you match.

61

- **Tinder** is the most well-known dating app and the most popular one globally. It's more hookup-oriented and it tends to be a little bit lower quality, although you can still meet some awesome women on it.

- **The League** is more of a premium dating app, focusing on young professional "high achievers." But you need to pass a bit of a rigorous screening process to get onto it, and so there's a lower volume of people. That said, there's definitely some quality women on there.

- **Raya** is similar to The League in that it requires users to apply for membership, and you're vetted based on different criteria. It's been known as the "celebrity dating app," as a lot of higher profile people are on it.

Honestly, I'd recommend starting with Hinge, Tinder, and Bumble. Put some effort into taking high-quality photos; don't just take random shots of your life. You really need to intentionally go out and take photos specifically for this—and if you can afford professional shots, that's the most ideal. If not, you can use portrait mode on your camera phone.

For pose, style, and background inspiration, check out our Beast Photos Instagram at //www.instagram.com/beastphotos_official/. These are the kinds of photos that are considered "top quality" and will get you plenty of matches and dates.

## The Power of Instagram

Even though it's not technically a dating app, Instagram is, in many ways, the best dating app at this point. It allows you to connect with women from all over the world, brand yourself as a high-quality guy, and solidify your interactions from dating apps and in-person conversations. Let's say that you're talking to a girl for two minutes, make a pretty good impression, and then close the conversation by getting her Instagram.

She doesn't have a ton to remember you by in the conversation, but when she takes a look at your Instagram profile later, she's blown away. You've got premium-looking photos, high-quality story highlights, and overall, it's clear that you know how to represent yourself well. She's going to be far more likely to want to follow through and hang out with you in this case, rather than if you had a bunch of awkward selfies and low-quality photos like most guys do.

Aside from building up your communication and flirting abilities, optimizing your Instagram and dating apps with great photos is the highest-leverage thing you can do. It can assert yourself as a top 5 to 10% man that women compete over, and it'll make all the strategies you'll discover in this book work even better.

Diving into the ins and outs of optimizing your Instagram is a bit out of the scope of this book, **but you can listen to me dive in-depth into it in this podcast episode:** https://spoti.fi/4389qP2.

**Key Takeaways**

- **Diversify Your Approach:** Don't rely solely on one method to meet women. Keep your options open and be adaptable to different environments and situations.

- **Daytime Opportunities:** Capitalize on everyday scenarios like the gym, grocery store, parks, malls, and downtown areas. These settings offer relaxed atmospheres conducive to starting conversations.

- **Nightlife Exploration:** While not everyone's jam, nightlife venues provide opportunities to meet a high volume of women in a small vicinity. Approach with an open mind and consider more intimate, low-key settings, and keep the drinking to a minimum (or just cut it out completely) so that you can stay socially sharp.

- **Online Dating:** Embrace the shift toward online dating platforms like Hinge, Bumble, and Tinder. Put effort into creating high-quality profiles with intentional photos to match with and date higher-quality women.

- **Instagram's Influence:** Leverage Instagram as a powerful dating tool. Optimize your profile with premium photos to stand out to top-tier women from both online and in-person conversations.

# What Good Flirting Looks Like

"I'm pretty good at talking to people, but women always tell me that they don't feel a connection. I don't get it!"

This is a really common thing I hear from guys who struggle with women. They often think that their dates and conversations are going well, but for some reason, women never seem to feel the same attraction.

Here's the thing: "Talking to people" at your work, within a friendship, or in your day-to-day life is *completely* different than flirting with a woman on a more seductive level. You can absolutely be amazing at the former and terrible at the latter.

And if you struggle to get girls out on dates, get past the first date, or move things forward with women in general, there's a good chance that your flirting ability (or lack thereof) is the culprit.

But once you fix that, you'll be able to spike a woman's attraction quite quickly and solve a lot of those mishaps.

The first step to fixing it is to understand what good flirting actually looks like, so let's dive in.

## It's Subtle Instead of Blunt

Flirting has a finesse to it. Think of it like leaving breadcrumbs instead of drawing a treasure map. Good flirting brings her into your world, but it also adds a little mystery and charm that's hard to resist. You don't let on that she fully has you—not just yet.

When you have the ability and patience to give her a sneak preview instead of the whole movie, it's powerful and it keeps her wanting more.

Here's some great ways to be subtle with your flirting. **You can use:**

- Body language cues. Maintain eye contact, smile warmly, lean in to convey your interest, and then back out to keep her wanting more.

- Innuendos. These can be a great way to imply something on the spicier side without outright saying it.

- Suggestive questions and assumptions to get her to open up.

  o **For example**, "You seem like the adventurous type."

## It's Playful Insead of Overly Serious

Flirting is also playful. This is a hard thing to grasp for many guys who take themselves so seriously in different aspects of life. But hey—this is *not* the time to be uptight.

Let's say that there's a woman in line in front of you at the coffee shop. Instead of diving straight into compliments about how beautiful she is, you have a playful exchange that keeps the mood light and intriguing.

"Decisions, decisions," you say with a grin as you nod toward the menu board.

She looks over and smiles, and you continue.

"I've been staring at the menu for a few minutes myself. Let me guess—you're more of a cappuccino girl, but you're feeling a little adventurous today?"

"How'd you know?" she laughs. "I might finally go for that pumpkin spice latte."

You raise an eyebrow playfully. "Stepping out of your comfort zone, huh? I like it," you say with a grin, appreciating her spontaneity. You've just turned a mundane conversation about coffee into a fun and playful one. And now it's easy to bridge the conversation from here into a new topic.

A simple exercise to be more playful in conversation is simply to think, "How can I make this a little more fun?" The goal isn't to be a Jack Black-style goofball—it's to add a little flavor into your conversations.

## It's Self-Assured Instead of Insecure

When you're confident in yourself and your intentions, you don't second guess every move you make while flirting. You know what you want and you're comfortable expressing it—whether it's showing interest, making a playful remark, or asking her out. This confidence allows you to flirt authentically without fear of rejection or judgment.

To be good at flirting, you need to do it from a place of self-amusement and genuine enjoyment—not because you're seeking validation or approval from the woman. You're not overly concerned with how she'll perceive it. If she vibes with your flirting style, great. If not, it might not be a good fit anyway (or you might just need to work a little more on your flirting ability).

This allows you to detach from the outcome, which leaves room to be more authentic, genuine, and fully present in the moment.

It provides a stark contrast with the men who are totally focused on trying to impress her, which usually comes off quite cringey. And you definitely don't want to be that guy.

## It Adds to the Connection

Flirting doesn't just add banter and fun to the interaction—it also adds to the connection.

You engage with her emotionally, and there's an element of vulnerability there as you both reveal different aspects about yourselves, your interests, and your senses of humor. Plus, it gives you the chance to develop inside jokes and playful gestures, as well as explore shared interests.

In essence, you bring her into your world for a few moments.

**For example, let's say that you're on a date with a girl and it goes something like this:**

**You:** (playfully nudging her arm) "So Kate, tell me—what's your secret talent? I bet you're hiding something impressive."

**Kate:** (laughs) "Hmm, well, I make a killer chocolate chip cookie. Does that count?"

**You:** (grinning) "Absolutely! Now, the *real* question is—when do I get to taste these legendary cookies?"

**Kate:** (teasingly) "Ah, that's the million-dollar question, isn't it? Maybe if you're lucky, I'll cook them for you one day."

**You:** "Consider me intrigued. Looks like I'll have to stick around to uncover the mystery. Just don't hate me if I unleash my inner Gordon Ramsey on your cookies."

You and Kate have some playful banter back and forth, and you're able to turn what could've been a potentially bland conversation about cookies into a flirty exchange that creates a sense of connection and mutual interest. Also, it hints at seeing each other again in the future.

## It's Risky…But Not Too Risky

Most guys are afraid to take risks in their conversations. Instead of seizing the opportunity to say something sexual or fun, they filter themselves and end up boring the girl. This usually results in an interview-mode conversation that leads nowhere.

"Where are you from?"

"How many brothers or sisters do you have?"

"What are your plans this weekend?"

If all you focus on is questions like these and never try to build off them to make things fun, your conversations will fall flat. Remember—it's okay to cross the line occasionally with something you say; this shows you where the line is! It also shows confidence.

And all good flirting comes with risk.

It involves putting yourself (and your humor) out there and being vulnerable. When you're expressing interest, making jokes, and adding in some physical touch, there's always a risk of misinterpretation or rejection, but you'll rarely get anywhere without taking those chances.

It also involves testing boundaries, whether through playful teasing or suggestive comments. This can create excitement and build attraction, but it also carries the risk of making her uncomfortable if not done tactfully.

However, all this comes with the territory, right? To be good at flirting, you *must* embrace the risk of it. After all, all good things lie on the other side of a good risk, so it's always better to be bold.

That being said, you don't need to take it all the way to the extreme. **You can take calculated risks while flirting, and here's how:**

- Read the room. Pay attention to her body language and verbal cues to gauge her interest and comfort level. If she seems receptive, you can gradually escalate things, and if she seems disinterested, you can dial it back.

- Start small. Begin with light-hearted banter and subtle compliments before diving into suggestive or intimate topics.

- Be genuine. Authenticity is key to successful flirting. Use flirting as a tool to express yourself and bring her in on the fun.

## Key Takeaways

- **Flirting Is Different from Regular Conversation:** Being good at chatting with friends doesn't automatically translate to successful flirting with women. Recognize that flirting involves a different dynamic and set of techniques.

- **Subtle and Playful:** Effective flirting is subtle rather than blunt. Inject playfulness into your interactions to keep the mood light and engaging. This can turn mundane conversations into enjoyable exchanges that build rapport.

- **Self-Assurance Is Key:** Confidence is attractive. Be comfortable expressing your intentions and interests without seeking validation from the woman. Detach from the outcome and focus on enjoying the interaction for what it is.

- **Deepen the Connection:** Good flirting goes beyond surface-level banter. It adds depth to the interaction by engaging with the woman emotionally and revealing shared interests and humor. Use it as a tool to bring her into your world and create a sense of connection and mutual interest.

- **Embrace Calculated Risks:** Flirting involves some level of risk. Start with small, light-hearted gestures and gradually escalate based on her interest level. Be genuine and authentic in your approach, and also be willing to take bold but calculated risks to build attraction.

# The Irresistible Flirting Techniques of Top 5% Men

You've now got a much deeper understanding of flirting and what attracts women, which means that you're equipped with a solid base.

Now let's examine some actual techniques that you can roll out in your conversations.

## Tonality

When it comes to flirting, it's not just about what you say—it's also about how you say it. Your tonality refers to your voice and overall manner of speaking, as well as how that adds (or subtracts) from the charm and effectiveness of your flirting.

Specifically, I'm referring to your pitch, pace, volume, inflection, expression, pausing, and emphasis. Let's flesh out how to get all these down the right way—otherwise, the rest of the techniques we'll cover will fall completely flat.

### Key Elements of Effective Tonality

#### 1. Speaking Slowly

Talking at a slower pace adds a sense of deliberation and confidence to your words. It allows her to absorb what you're saying, creating a sense of intimacy and significance.

Most guys talk about two to three times faster than they should when communicating with women. As a general rule, you should slow it down until you feel like it's a little *too* slow. It may seem a bit weird at first, but that's probably the right pace!

## 2. Low-Pitched Tone

Women *love* men with deeper voices. A lower tone of voice conveys a sense of calm and confidence. Avoiding uptalk, which is when your voice rises at the end of sentences, is crucial. Keeping your tone even or slightly downward at the end of sentences makes you seem more certain.

**Below are a few tips to speak with a lower-pitched voice:**

- **Relax Your Throat:** When your throat is tense, it can actually constrict your voice and make it higher. Try to relax your throat muscles, as this leads to a deeper, fuller sound.

- **Breath Control:** Breathe deeply from your diaphragm (the muscle just below your rib cage) rather than your chest. This type of breathing supports a stronger and deeper voice.

- **Lower Your Pitch Gradually:** Start speaking at your natural pitch, and then gradually lower it to a comfortable level. Avoid straining your voice—the goal here is to sound deeper while still sounding natural.

- **Mindful Speaking:** Be aware of your voice during conversations. If you notice your pitch rising due to excitement or nerves, take a moment to pause and re-adjust.

- **Record and Listen:** Recording your voice and listening back can provide insight into your natural tone and areas for improvement.

I have my clients do this all the time so that we can point out and adjust the weak points of their tonality.

- **Voice Exercises:** Try these to strengthen your vocal cords.

    o **For example**, you can hum at different pitches, starting higher and then going lower, to find your natural deep tone.

### 3. Facial Expressions & The Sexy Smile

Your facial expressions should complement your tonality. A genuine, warm smile or a subtle, playful smirk can make your words more powerful.

You can also break out the "sexy smile"—this is a subtle, knowing smile, with minimal teeth showing and a light squint. Ryan Gosling's character Jacob in Crazy, Stupid, Love often uses this technique, so check some clips to get an idea.

### 4. Relaxed & Playful Attitude

You want to convey a laid-back, easygoing attitude through your voice, as it makes the conversation feel light and enjoyable. It also shows you're comfortable and enjoying the interaction, which makes her more relaxed, too.

### 5. Matching Energy Levels

Part of effective tonality is adapting to the energy of the conversation. If she's speaking with excitement, slightly increase your energy level to match hers. In more intimate or serious moments, a softer, lower tone can create a sense of closeness.

## 6. The Power of Pauses

Well-timed pauses can add emphasis to your words, create suspense, or give space for her to add to the conversation. They make you sound more interesting and your words seem more captivating.

One of my favorite ways to use pauses is on the approach.

**For example,** "Hey…I know this is super, super random…but I saw you…and I thought you were stunning…and I had to meet you for a minute…I'm Dave." These pauses in between certain parts of what you're saying to her can be irresistible and leave her hanging on your words.

## 7. Volume Control

Adjust your volume to suit the environment. In quieter settings, use a softer, more inviting tone. In louder settings, speak clearly and loudly to make sure that she hears you.

## Practical Application in Flirting Scenarios

- During a date, if she shares something personal with you, respond with a softer, empathetic tone and a gentle smile to show understanding and interest.

- When using playful banter, use a slightly quicker pace and a more animated tone, paired with expressive facial gestures, to keep the energy lively.

- When giving a compliment or asking a flirty question, slow down and lower your pitch slightly to add sincerity and depth to your words.

# Teasing

Teasing is when you make fun of a girl in a playful manner. It's basically a mix of witty banter that adds a little twist to the conversation, all while keeping it respectful and light. You never insult her—it's more like poking innocent fun.

**Let's look at a few examples of teasing in action below.**

**Her:** "I'm really into astrology."

**Good tease:** "Oh, wow—you're totally a libra, aren't you? This is never gonna work."

**Bad tease:** "You believe in that stuff? Sounds pretty superstitious to me."

**Her:** "I love to cook. "

**Good tease:** "Oh, a chef, huh? So, when you say 'cooking,' are we talking gourmet meals or expert-level grilled cheese?"

**Bad tease:** "I knew it—you belong in the kitchen."

**Her:** "I love Game of Thrones."

**Good tease:** "Yeah, I'm kinda getting Cersei vibes from you, actually."

**Bad tease:** "Wow, you're such a nerd, aren't you?"

**Here's how you can tease effectively:**

- **Read Her Responses:** How does she react to your teasing? If she laughs or teases back, it's a good sign. If she shuts down or seems uncomfortable, it's time to pull back.

- **Keep It Light:** Teasing should be light and respectful. Avoid sensitive topics like religion, politics, appearance, style, or personal issues.

- **Back-and-Forth Banter:** Teasing is a two-way street—you both should be getting in on the fun. This creates a fun and playful interaction, and it shows that you can dish it out as well as you can take it.

- **Don't Self-Deprecate:** Do this too often, and you'll come off like you lack confidence.

- **Make sure that your tonality is on point:** Smile when you tease, use a light tone, and make sure it's clear that you're being playful.

- **Don't Lay It on Too Thick:** Sometimes guys get carried away and tease her too much. Keep a balance between teasing, other flirting styles, and actually getting to know her.

# Passing Her Tests

Women—especially quality women—are going to test you often, especially early on in the dating process. She tests you because she wants to see that you are who you say you are. Can you hold up against a little pushback, or do you fold at the first sign of pressure?

When she tests you, it's actually a *good* thing. She's rooting for you to pass and to give her a reason to be more interested. And then it's on you where to take it.

One of the best ways to pass her tests is to agree and exaggerate. This is when you take what she says, amplify it humorously, and show her that you're not easily fazed. It keeps the conversation fun and playful rather than turning it into a serious discussion (and you failing the test).

Another good way is to put it back on her. This is where you playfully turn the statement back in her direction, create a playful back-and-forth dynamic, and essentially give her the same test.

## Let's look at a few examples of this in action:

**Her:** "Just so you know, I don't sleep with guys on the first date."

**Exaggerate:** "Thank God, because I'm saving myself for marriage."

**Back on her:** "You're getting a little ahead of yourself here. You need to wine and dine me first."

**Bad:** "Don't worry! I'd never try that tonight."


**Her:** "I normally don't date guys your age."

**Exaggerate:** "Fair enough. I'm actually 85 at heart. I just work out a lot and have an exceptional skincare routine."

**Back on her:** "That's okay. I'll slow down a little so that you can keep up."

**Bad:** "Age is just a number. It's not a big deal!"

**Her:** "You probably say that to every girl."

**Exaggerate:** "Of course. I've got it scripted and everything. You're right at the point where you're charmed and intrigued."

**Back on her:** "Right, and you're the mysterious one who's heard it all before. Quite the dynamic we have here."

**Bad:** "I don't say this to other girls, I swear!"

# Misinterpretation

This is when you playfully misconstrue something she says as an advance or innuendo. Again, you want to keep it light here and slightly suggestive without crossing the line into being vulgar or offensive.

The point is to add a playful spin to the conversation and position yourself as the prize. It can be great as well for getting more "innocent" girls to start showing you their "not-so-innocent" side. And, as with all flirting, subtlety is key.

**Below, some examples of misinterpretation:**

**Her:** "Oh my God, I love dancing!"

**Good:** "You must have good rhythm then, huh? That's important for a lot of things."

**Bad:** "You must be really good in bed then." (too vulgar)

**Her:** "I'm really into yoga."

**Good:** "Yoga, huh? I've always admired flexibility—in *all* aspects of life."

**Bad:** "Wow, I bet you can bend in some interesting ways." (too suggestive)

**Her:** (early on in a date) "I actually live across the street from here."

**Good:** "Wow, slow down! At least buy me a drink before you invite me over."

**Bad:** "Let's go there right now." (too forward and fast)

What's good about misinterpretation is that it can give you a sense of where you stand with her. If she plays along or even takes that line of conversation to a further level, there's a solid chance that she has high interest in you. If she's neutral, it's still a good sign because at least she's not shutting it down. But if she *does* shut it down completely, you've got some work to do.

## Push/Pull

Push/pull is a flirting technique in which you balance showing interest (the pull) and playfully teasing or feigned disinterest (the push). This creates intrigue, leaves her wanting more, and sparks interest.

## Understanding Push/Pull

The pull draws her closer emotionally, often through compliments, expressions of interest, or showing a deeper level of investment. Basically, it signals attraction.

The push, in contrast, creates a playful challenge or barrier, usually through teasing, light-hearted criticism, or playful disinterest. It adds an element of unpredictability to the interaction.

## The following are some examples of push/pull in action:

**Her:** "Really? I hate sushi."

**Push:** "I can't believe you don't like sushi! This is never going to work."

**Her:** "Yeah, such a bummer."

**Pull:** "Well, good thing you're kinda cute. Maybe I can look past the sushi."

**Pull:** "I really respect that you prioritize your fitness."


**Her:** "Thank you! I've been going hard lately."

**Push:** "Let me feel you flex real quick. (hold her bicep area) Okay, you can flex now." (the joke is that you act like you can't tell that she's flexing when she actually is)

**You:** "Let's go back to my place (pull), but only if you promise not to make any moves on me (push)."

There's also a non-verbal side to push/pull. This is all about body language, and opening and closing the space between the two of you. If you weave this into your interactions the right way, she'll begin to crave your touch and want to get closer to you.

## Below are some ways you can push/pull non-verbally:

### 1. Lean In and Out During the Conversation

**Pull:** Leaning in during an important or intimate part of the conversation signals interest and creates a moment of closeness. This is easy to do at louder nighttime venues, where you can lean in and talk in her ear for a moment, and then lean back out again.

**Push:** Leaning out slightly after sharing a moment of laughter or an interesting point in the conversation creates a temporary space between you and makes her miss your touch.

### 2. Arm Gestures

**Push:** Casually placing your arm around her for a minute and then naturally pulling away adds a layer of comfort and spontaneity. She knows that you're comfortable doing it without being overbearing.

**Pull:** The initial act of putting your arm around her is a warm, inviting gesture that can work well when used sparingly.

### 3. Dance Dynamics

**Push:** While the two of you are dancing, intentionally creating a little space after a close move adds an element of playfulness. You're not "all up in her grill" for too long that it makes her uncomfortable. You're able to let it breathe.

**Pull:** Dancing closely, especially during a slow or romantic song, establishes a physical connection and intimacy.

(Note: Reggaeton is *perfect* for this. This style of music makes it easy to dance close, back away, then come back in close again. And actually, Latin dancing in general makes this quite easy if you have a little rhythm.)

## 4. Tease the Kiss

**Push:** Lean in as if thinking of kissing her and building anticipation, but then gently pull back, prolonging the moment and increasing her desire. She *knows* that you know that you can get it, and you both know that you're going to do it—you're just playfully making her wait for it.

**Pull:** The initial lean-in, paired with slow talking and eye contact, creates a magnetic pull that draws her into the moment.

You can also do this with an actual kiss, but this is actually where many guys screw up. Once they get a kiss, they go for a full-on, ten-minute makeout. You might think that this is a win but it kills *all* the tension—especially after what may have been a solid first date.

There's a time and a place for long makeouts—generally when you're somewhere private where intimacy is possible. Otherwise, it over-validates her, creates too much "pull," and actually makes her less excited to see you again (and yes—if this sounds familiar, the long makeout session by your car may have been why you didn't get that second date).

What's far better is to use push/pull with the actual kiss—kiss her for three to five seconds and then be the first one to pull back. You can do this several times throughout the interaction. It's never enough to fully validate her, but just enough to spike the tension and leave her wanting more.

Then, once you're eventually back in private, the built-up tension can lead to a passionate night.

## 5. Playful Touches

**Push:** Lightly touch her arm or shoulder during the flow of conversation and then pull your hand back. You can also put your hand on her leg or around her waist for a few moments before pulling it back. This makes her comfortable with your touch and gets her craving more of it.

**Pull:** Initiating these light touches expresses interest and creates a connection.

## 6. Eye Contact Dynamics

**Push:** Breaking eye contact after a shared laugh or a moment of connection leaves her wanting more.

**Pull:** Holding eye contact during key parts of the conversation indicates deep interest and connection.

Here's the best way to think about flirty eye contact: As you look into her eyes, you have the mindset of, "This is fun, and I know you're into it," and also, "You're sexy, but let's see what else you've got."

It's like a playful little game of cat and mouse. You both understand what's going on—and you're both enjoying it.

## 7. Adjusting Space

**Push:** Occasionally adjusting your position to create a bit of distance can build intrigue and make her more inclined to close the gap.

**Pull:** Closing the space, like when moving in to share something private, creates a sense of exclusivity and intimacy.

# Future Projecting

This term describes a flirting technique in which you create fun, fictional scenarios about future adventures or experiences with the person you're flirting with. It's a perfect way to transition from simply having a fun and flirty conversation to creating a sense of possibility and togetherness.

## The Art of Future Projecting

**Creating Shared Scenarios:** These scenarios involve both of you in an imagined future that's enjoyable and exciting. It's a way of subtly suggesting compatibility and shared interests while indicating that this conversation could actually lead somewhere.

**Building a Connection:** By talking about shared future experiences, you're not only deepening the rapport but also planting seeds for potential future dates or interactions.

## When to Use Future Projecting:

- **After Building Rapport:** It's best used once you've established a connection and she's showing interest. Jumping into future projecting too early can come off as presumptuous.

- **Align with Her Interests:** If she mentions a hobby or a dream, like traveling to Asia or learning salsa dancing, use that information to build your scenario.

- **Detail-Oriented:** Adding details helps her to visualize and engage with the scenario more vividly.

- **Inclusive Language:** Use "we" to make it inclusive and create a sense of togetherness.

Below are some examples of future projecting in action:

**Traveling Together Scenario:**

**Her:** "I've always wanted to visit Asia."

**You:** "Me too—imagine us exploring the streets of Tokyo, getting things lost in translation and laughing about it, and finding the best sushi spot in the city. But I have to warn you that I take my karaoke seriously."

**Learning a New Skill Together:**

**Her:** "I've always wanted to learn salsa dancing."

**You:** "We'd crush it on the dance floor. I can picture us now—gracefully out of sync at first, but soon after that, we're the stars of the dancefloor. Just promise that you won't outshine me on the first lesson."

**Sharing A Fun Experience Together:**

**Her:** "I've always wanted to try skydiving."

**You:** "Okay, that's it then—we're going skydiving. You handle the screaming and I'll handle the courage. We'll just freefall and hope for the best. *You're* doing the mid-air backflips, though."

The key with future projecting is to keep it hypothetical. If you try to actually make specific plans, it ruins the fun, creates a weird dynamic, and immediately makes you seem like a guy who "doesn't get it." Basically, you don't want to use the skydiving joke and then say, "Oh, I know this skydiving school we can go to! Does next Saturday work for you?" Instead, you keep her skydiving dreams in mind for a future date and then bring it up later on if you guys continue to hang out.

# Flirty Questions

These are fun and easy tools that you can break out to spice up your dates and interactions. They create sexual tension, shift things to a more flirty mood, and give you insights into her preferences and personality.

### Setting the Stage for Flirty Questions

- **Timing:** These questions work best once you've built a little rapport—launching into them too early might seem abrupt or uncalibrated.

- **Reading the Room:** Gauge her comfort level and response to your initial conversation. If she seems open and engaged, it's a good sign for you to introduce flirty questions.

### Types of Flirty Questions

- **Light and Playful:** These are questions that are fun and easy to answer, which sets a lighthearted mood.

**Some examples:**

- o "If you could have any superpower for just one day, what would it be…and would you use it to woo me?"

- o "If you could wake up anywhere in the world tomorrow, where would it be?"

- **A Bit Provocative:** These are slightly edgier questions that tread into the territory of flirtation and attraction, and they're designed to build sexual tension.

**Some examples:**

- o "What's something that always turns your head when you see a guy?"

- o "What do you find sexiest in a guy?"

- o "What was your last crazy adventure?"

- o "What's the worst first date you've ever been on?" (The great thing about this is that it's a loaded question—it assumes that the date she's on with you right now is a good one!)

- **Personal but Intriguing:** These questions allow her to share more about herself in a playful context.

**Some examples:**

- o "What's one thing that I wouldn't guess about you?"

- o "What kinds of things make you laugh the hardest?"

- o "What did you want to be when you grew up?"

## Responding to Her Answers

When it comes to responding, you can mix your genuine thoughts with a bit of fun and playfulness. This can help springboard the conversation into something deeper, and you can weave in and out between light flirting and deeper topics.

**For example,** let's say you ask her, "What do you find sexiest in a guy?"

**Her:** "I love when a guy is confident and has a great sense of humor. Lookswise? Dark hair, blue eyes, and a great smile." (And if she likes you, she'll typically describe *you* when she answers this question, which is always awesome!)

**You:** "Okay, so you like to keep it light and have some fun. I like that—I'm the same way. Can't take yourself too seriously. (smiling) Blue eyes and dark hair though, huh?" (assuming that those things describe you)

**Her:** (laughs) "Yeah, you caught me. What about you—what do you like in a girl?"

From here, if you like her, you can lightly describe her in return, along with some qualities you'd like her to embody. She'll often start trying to prove that she *has* these qualities.

**You:** "Well, I like girls with long brown hair and good style…girls who are independent and have a little bit of an adventurous side. You know—girls who don't care what people think all that much."

**Her:** "Oh, yeah? Well, I guess I have a little bit of an adventurous side…"

**You:** (smiling) "I'll have to see that for myself…"

## Key Takeaways

- **Tonality - The Secret Sauce:** Slow down the pace of your speaking and drop your voice a notch—you'll project confidence with every word. And don't forget that smirk or sexy smile—it adds flavor to what you're saying and helps you convey the right vibe.

- **Teasing - Keep It Fun, Not Insulting:** Tease her like you're in on a private joke together. It's not about taking digs—it's about playful banter that gets her smiling. Watch her reactions; if she's laughing and firing back, you're golden.

- **Passing Her Tests:** When she throws you a curveball, hit it out of the park by agreeing and exaggerating. Show her that her little tests don't faze you. Keep it light, keep it fun, and keep it moving.

- **Master Push/Pull:** Draw her in both physically and verbally with genuine interest, then toss a bit of a challenge her way with a mix of savvy banter and the right body language (like dancing up close, then further away, and repeating).

- **Future Projecting and Planting a Seed of Adventure:** Spin tales about adventures that you could have together. It's not planning—it's fantasizing out loud. These are like "us against the world" scenarios. Make her laugh—and make her wonder, "What if?"

- **Spice Things Up with Flirty Questions:** Once you've got a good rhythm going, pop in some flirty questions. Keep it spicy but not too heavy, and you'll get a sense for how open she is (and how willing she is to play into innuendos and "sexier" topics).

- **Strike the Balance:** All this flirting is great, but don't forget to mix in some real talk, too. It's not just about being the fun guy— he's forgettable. When you're fun *and* real, she won't be able to stop thinking about you.

# Part 3

# How to Flirt in Key Situations

# How to Flirt When You First Meet Her

You see a girl and you want to talk to her. Now what?

This isn't about walking up to her and throwing a pickup line her way. It's about kicking off the interaction with a solid vibe and creating a spark.

Let's talk about how to start this off with a bang and not a fizzle. When it comes to initiating the conversation, you've got a few great options, which we'll explore below.

## Situational Openers: Your Environment Is Your Wingman

These openers involve you using your surroundings as a launchpad for the conversation. The nice part about these is that they can feel a little smoother, and they also demonstrate that you can be observant and quick on your feet.

Basically, you're showing her that you're not just another guy with a line—you're someone who can turn an everyday moment into something a bit more exciting. Plus, it's a low-pressure way to gauge her interest. If she bites and plays along, you're in good shape. If not, no big deal—you just keep it moving.

# Let's look at a few examples of flirty situational openers:

## Grocery Store Gambit

Picture this perfect setup: You're both eyeing the avocados. Roll in with something like, "Ever feel like choosing the right avocado is like defusing a bomb? Pick the wrong one and your guac's a goner." Something like this is effective because it's relatable, everyday stuff but you're making it fun.

## Gym Tactics

Maybe she's trying a new machine during her workout. Slide in with, "That machine's a beast, right? I swear it's half workout and half puzzle trying to figure it out."

What's the winning angle here? You're in the same boat, and it's a shared challenge.

## Park Play

Maybe you see her at the park and she's reading or jogging. A comment like, "That book any good? I'm on the hunt for my next park bench read" can work wonders. The edge here is that you're showing interest in her taste, and it's a great segue into deeper topics.

## The Drink Observation

Let's say she's at the bar trying to decide what to order, or maybe she's just received an unusual-looking drink. Lean in (not too close—mind her personal space) with a hint of a smile and say something like, "That drink looks like it has a story behind it. Is it as good as it looks or are you just being adventurous tonight?"

# Non-Situational Openers: Straight Shooting

Sometimes the situation itself doesn't give you much to work with, especially in fast-paced environments like a busy street or a lively festival.

This is where non-situational openers come into play. They're about diving in with either a direct or an indirect approach and cutting through the noise—you're making your intentions clear but in a smooth and calibrated way.

## The Direct Approach

A direct opener is straight-forward and leaves no room for ambiguity. It's a clear, confident approach in which you're expressing your interest from the start.

**Let's look at some examples:**

**Compliment-Based:** "Excuse me, I just noticed you from across the room and had to say that your sense of style is amazing. I'm (your name)."

**Interest Declaration:** "Hey, I know this might be random, but I saw you standing here and felt compelled to come over and meet you. I'm (your name)."

What makes the direct opener effective is that it shows confidence and honesty, and it sets the tone for the interaction.

This works best in situations where social interaction isn't expected, like walking down the street, at a park, and in other everyday situations. Not at the gym though—if you use the direct approach there, you'll quickly come across as "that guy" hitting on every girl. Stick to a situational approach in that environment.

That said, direct openers can also work decently well in situations where social interaction is expected, like bars and lounges. Usually they're not as needed there, as you have so much situational fodder to use—but if you spot a total knockout and feel compelled to go direct, go for it.

# Nightlife Openers

Let's quickly cover some more openers you can use in nightlife settings when there's a bit more stimulation and it might be hard to hold full conversations. **A few examples:**

**Situational**

If she's at the bar: "What's your go-to drink? I want to try something new tonight."

Around the edge of the dancefloor/at the bar: "What do you think about the music here? Are you a big reggaeton/hip hop/pop fan?"

**The "Dance Floor Hip Bump"**

On the dancefloor: Give her a playful hip bump, smile, and take a step back. If she smiles back at you, gently take her hand, spin her, and start dancing. **To help you visualize this, check out an example of me doing the dance floor hip bump here:** https://bit.ly/hip-bump-flirting.

### The "She's Leaving"

Use this one when it appears that she's about to leave the venue and it's your last shot:

"Hey, I just noticed you and I had to meet you quickly before you go." This can be great for grabbing quick phone numbers and shooting your shot before you miss your chance.

# Weaving In Banter Early On

Banter is the playful, witty exchange that adds a spark to your interactions. It can help transition the conversation from boring small talk to something more fun and flirty, breaking through the initial awkwardness.

You want to start weaving this in after the initial conversation starter.

### How to Weave in Banter

Let's look at some ways that you can weave banter into the early part of your interactions:

### Guessing Her Origin or Background

You can start with a playful guess about where she might be from or what her background is. This is a great way to show interest without directly asking, and regardless of whether you get it right, it makes things more fun.

### Some examples:

- "You have a vibe that's hard to pin down, but I'm getting strong West Coast energy. Or maybe I'm just hoping you'll say that you're from somewhere with great surf."

- "You don't strike me as someone who's spent their life just in one place. You've got a big 'city girl' kind of vibe."

- "I'm usually good with accents, but yours has me stumped. It's not quite local but not quite foreign either. I'm guessing you're not from around here, are you?"

## Guessing Her Profession

Not only does this add a spark of intrigue to your conversation but it also provides insight into her world. It's a playful way to demonstrate interest in her that goes beyond surface-level small talk.

**Some examples:**

- "You have an artistic flair about you. I'm getting strong graphic designer vibes, or maybe an architect? Definitely something that lets you channel creativity."

  o **Why It Works:** It shows that you're paying attention to her style and mannerisms, attributing them to creative and intellectually stimulating professions.

- "There's a decisiveness in your eye. I'm torn between thinking you're a lawyer who's always three steps ahead or a CEO running her own startup."

  o **Why It Works:** This guess attributes qualities of leadership and intelligence to her, which can be flattering and thought provoking.

If you're in more of a nightlife setting, you can incorporate the surroundings to fuel your banter. **Examples:**

- "You like vodka? I can't believe it. I'm a tequila guy—this'll never work!"

  o **Why It Works:** It adds a playful little "push," which can be used in a push/pull dynamic.

- "Your drink choice says a lot about you. That looks like a 'taking over the world one sip at a time' kind of cocktail."

  o **Why It Works:** It's a fun way to comment on her drink choice while subtly complimenting her confidence or ambition.

# Getting Her Contact Info

You've started the conversation and had some solid banter, and now you're in a good position to close things out and get her contact info.

Daytime interactions, like a chance meeting at the park or a quick chat in the coffee line, are typically brief. You're both on-the-go, so it's short and sweet (maybe one to five minutes). Recognizing the tempo of the interaction is key for properly getting her contact info.

**The Setup**

When the conversation reaches a natural high point and you're feeling that mutual vibe, it's time to pivot to the close. Start with something like, "Hey, I've got to meet a friend, but you seem like fun. Do you want to hang out sometime?"

If she says no, just say, "All good—take it as a compliment."

If she says yes, hand her your phone on the contact entry screen and say, "Cool. Add your number here and we'll make it happen."

Or, if you have an optimized Instagram (if you're not sure if it's optimized, then it's not—you can't "luck" your way into an attractive IG), you can opt for getting her IG instead. In this case, it's actually better if *you* put it into her phone.

Once she agrees, the way to do it is to say, "Cool. Here—search my IG"—you can type it yourself or have her type it. Ideally you're typing it, and you can just go in, follow yourself, and then drop yourself a quick direct message (like an emoji) from her account. That way, she'll immediately see your message when you DM her, and it won't go to the "Message Requests" tab.

You'll want to get her contact info in the first interaction every time, *except* for situations where you know that you're very likely to see her again.

**For example**, at the gym when you two typically go on the same days or times, or at a dance class where you see each other once a week or a few times a month.

In cases like those, it's okay to build rapport the first time and then go for the contact info on your second or third conversation when she shows signs of interest. This helps you uphold your reputation and be a little more calculated.

## Closing Out Nightlife Interactions

Nightlife scenarios, in contrast, can be brief at the beginning of the night when you're first building momentum. You might have three or four quick interactions of a few minutes (or even less), where you end by exchanging contact info.

But as the night progresses, you'll typically find yourself in longer interactions. In these cases, it's key to weave in the flirting that's been throughout this book. You also want to lead and "make it real."

Making it real means making a genuine connection beyond just the fun flirting. And yes—there *is* time to do this in nightlife interactions. Generally, it's best to take her to a quieter part of the venue where you can talk a little deeper and get to know her without all the crazy loud music. This will solidify the interaction more and make it a more memorable experience for her, and it's key if you want to minimize the chances of her flaking or ghosting you the next day.

**To make it real, you can ask questions like:**

- "What brought you to this city?"

- "What do you like to do for fun?"

- "What was your last big adventure?"

- "If you could wake up anywhere in the world tomorrow, where would it be?"

When she poses the questions back to you, you can relate with quick stories about your own life before turning the conversation back over to her.

And when it comes to leading, I'm referring to guiding the interaction from beginning to end toward your desired outcome. You can do things like move her throughout different parts of the venue, like the dancefloor, the bar, and quieter areas. The more she follows your lead, the more invested she becomes in the interaction, allowing you to make bigger asks.

**To properly lead well, do the following:**

- Know where you're going. Have a desired outcome in mind.

- Know your logistics—where you're staying, when you need to wake up, and how you'll get home.

- Build compliance. Basically, this refers to when a girl does what you want her to be doing.

    o **For example,** if you stop her to talk and she stops and listens, or if you lead her somewhere and she follows. You can give her "compliance tests" like these throughout the interaction to get an idea of where you stand.

**Let's look at a few examples of leading in action:**

- Grabbing a drink with her: "You're fun. Let's go grab a drink at the bar."

- Taking her to the lounge area for easier conversation: "Let's go hang out in the lounge—it's super chill over there."

- Going out for fresh air: "Let's get outside for a second—it's kinda stuffy in here."

- The dance floor to get a little more physical: "This song is awesome—let's hit the dance floor."

- You can also simply hold her hand as you lead her through a crowd.

Keep in mind that by going for the smaller asks (like "Let's go to the dance floor"), you give yourself a better chance to get a "yes" for the bigger asks (such as "Let's go back to my place").

If she shuts down your first few compliance tests, consider moving on. In those cases, it saves you time and allows you to meet other girls who you *will* click with.

As far as closing in nightlife scenarios goes, if you're going for the contact info, you can use the same kind of ask as the daytime close. It just might be a longer interaction and therefore more solidified (if you've done things right).

If you're looking to keep the night going at your place or hers and you leave the venue together, the following are some easy phrases to use (but make sure that you've built a good amount of compliance before trying them):

### The Simple "Crazy, Stupid, Love" Close

**You:** "Do you want to get out of here?

**Her:** "Sure."

This seems simple, but if she likes you, if she's invested in the interaction, and if you've led well, she'll be more open to it than you think.

### The "Adventure" Close

**You:** "Let's get out of here."

**Her:** "Okay, what do you want to do?"

**You:** "You up for an adventure?"

**Her**: "Yes."

**You:** "Cool—follow me."

Then go outside together, let her know that you live nearby, and call an Uber or a taxi.

## The "Let's Get Food" Close

Maybe the night's coming to an end, but you can tell that she's not quite ready to go somewhere more private yet. That's when it helps to have a "bridge" location that allows you to switch venues and build more rapport. The simple way to do this is go for food after the bar—something quick like a slice or two of pizza is perfect. From there, you can invite her to somewhere private. You can initiate this with something like:

**You:** "There's a great pizza joint down the street. You want to grab a slice?"

**Her:** "Sure!"

## Key Takeaways

- **Leverage Your Environment:** Use situational openers to start conversations—they feel smoother and demonstrate your ability to be observant and quick-witted.

- **Adapt to the Context:** The approach you use can vary based on where you are. For everyday settings like streets or parks, direct openers can be more effective, as they show confidence and clarity. In social environments like bars or clubs, situational openers can help you break the ice.

- **Banter is Key:** Early on in the interaction, weave in playful banter. An example of this could be guessing her background or profession in a light-hearted way.

- **Close with Confidence:** Unless you know that you're likely to see her again (like in a gym setting), go for the contact info in the first interaction. Ask if she wants to hang out sometime, and then get her number or exchange Instagram accounts (but only if your IG is optimized).

- **Know When and How to Lead:** Especially in longer nightlife interactions, it's key to lead the interaction purposefully. This includes moving her through different parts of the venue and building compliance with smaller requests before making larger ones, like suggesting heading back to your place or hers.

# How to Flirt on Dates

Think about it: First-date flirting is actually the easiest kind. Why? She's already there with you. That means that she saw something in you—a spark, a hint of intrigue—something that made her think, "Yeah, this could be interesting. "

She's stepped into the ring with you, and that's half the battle won. This isn't a cold call; it's more like being handed a warm lead. At this point, it's not about proving your worth from square one—it's about building on the intrigue that's already there.

Let's examine how to make the most of it, have a solid first date, and infuse great flirting skills along the way.

## The Goals of a First Date

First dates are basically a testing ground to see if you have chemistry with a girl. With this in mind, there are four goals:

### 1. Get Clarity on Compatibility

Sure, she caught your eye—but does she catch your vibe? Use this opportunity to see if there's more than just physical attraction. Does the conversation flow? Do your values align? Is there a spark when you share stories and ideas? Do you want the same things? Or does it all feel a little flat and forced?

And, most of all, is it worth a second date to continue getting to know each other?

## 2. Make It Cost-Effective

The point of becoming skilled at flirting isn't to go on five dates a week—it's to be able to easily have fun interactions, attract women, and be in control of your dating life. That said, you may actually *want* five dates every week, which is great, or you might be content with just a few dates a month, and that's fine too. The point is that you're able to achieve what you want.

With that in mind, if you're going on dates somewhat often, you need to make it sustainable. A $200 dinner date a few nights a week (or month) probably won't be worth it—nor is it necessary.

Instead, make your dates cost-effective. Opt for venues and date ideas that allow for solid conversation without the pressure of racking up an expensive bill. You can save that Michelin-starred restaurant for when she's actually your girlfriend.

## 3. Enjoy the Date & Have Fun!

If you're not enjoying yourself, what's the point? The goal is to enjoy each other's company. After all, this isn't a job interview—it's a chance to connect and have a good time.

Find joy in the little things during the date: a funny observation, a shared interest, or a quirky anecdote—all the things that are involved with getting to know somebody new. This can create a memorable experience for both of you.

Plus, you get a chance to try some of the new flirting techniques you learned here in this book, and that's a win!

## 4. Set the Stage for More

Whether it's another date or something more casual, leave the door open for future interactions. First dates aren't always about finding "The One"—sometimes they're just about exploring what could be. Yes, there's the possibility that she could be your next girlfriend. Or maybe she's cool but you don't click on a romantic level, and she could actually introduce you to her *friend* who becomes your next girlfriend! Or maybe it's more of a casual hookup situation. Keep your mind and your options open.

# Cheap & Simple First Date Ideas

To accomplish those four goals above, you don't need to have some kind of amazing first date idea. In fact, there are only really two first date ideas you should have in your arsenal, except for some rare exceptions.

## 1. The Bar Date

Bars provide a perfect first date atmosphere—as long as you choose the right one.

You want a venue where you can hear each other but still feel the buzz of the nightlife. The right bar sets a mood that's casual yet intimate, a vibe that's perfect for getting to know each other without the pressure.

And if you don't drink? No problem. I don't drink anymore either. You can go somewhere with mocktails so that you can avoid the alcohol but still enjoy the benefits of the vibe.

Bonus points if the bar has a billiards table or darts—these give you an extra activity and are an easy way to lead her around the venue and get to know her more.

The ideal time for bar dates is weeknights starting from around 7 or 8 pm. It's not as packed as on a weekend but there should still be a decent crowd, setting the tone for a chill evening.

Choose a bar on the cheaper side (or one with daily drink discounts) if you're going on lots of dates so that you can keep costs low.

### 2. The Coffee & a Walk Date

This is an easy, chill, and inexpensive date idea if you want to mix in some daytime dates.

An ideal coffee shop has an easy-going vibe, and it's a perfect place to start. It's low investment, both in time and money, which makes saying yes easy for her, too. Plus, coffee offers a laid-back setting to get the date rolling.

Post-coffee, take the date outside. A walk through a bustling downtown area or a stroll by the lake gives you a cool backdrop for your date. It keeps things moving, both literally and conversationally.

## Flirting on the First Date

Start off by greeting her outside the venue with a warm smile and a genuine but quick hug—this sets the tone for the rest of the date.

Then lead her into the venue, and once inside, sit next to her rather than across from her. This makes it easier to flirt and use physical touch, and it makes it feel less like an interview.

Once you're settled in, you can start rolling out some of the conversations and flirting strategies laid out earlier in this book.

## Make It Flirty from the Start

You can ask something simple like, "How's your day been?" or "How was the drive here?" Her answers may give you opportunities to drop a few light, playful teases right away.

**For example:**

**"How's your day been so far?"** Her: (explains a busy day filled with a bunch of activities) You: "Wow—you've been crushing it today, huh? I might need to take notes."

**Her:** (explains a relaxed day) You: "Keeping it Zen, huh? We're going to have to add a little excitement into your days."

**"How was your drive in?"** Her: (talks about all the traffic) You: : "You survived city traffic without losing your cool? I'm impressed!"

**Her:** (says it was a smooth drive) You: "Look at you, dodging traffic. I might need to take you with me on my drive to work."

## Dive Deep & Sprinkle in Some Flirting

Once you get past some of the initial pleasantries and teasing, you can get to know her a bit.

Below are some example questions you can ask:

**Exploring Her Background:**

- "What was your favorite thing about growing up in (her hometown)?"

- "If you could bring one aspect of your hometown here, what would it be?"

- "What's one thing you miss about your hometown?"

- "What brought you here in the first place?"

- (if you both grew up in the same city) "What made you want to stick around?"

## Understanding Her Career Choices:

- "Was working in (her field) always your plan, or did you stumble into it by chance?"

- "What got you interested in your field?"

- "What do you enjoy most about what you do?"

- "If you weren't doing this, what would be your dream job?"

## Getting to Know Her Hobbies and Passions

- "What kinds of things are you most passionate about?"

- "What makes you so passionate about (her passion)?"

- "How do you feel when you're following that passion?"

- "What do you like to do for fun?"

- "What do you love about (what she loves to do)?"

## Travel & Adventure

- "If you could wake up anywhere in the world tomorrow, where would it be?"

- "What's your favorite travel story?"

- "What's your favorite travel destination you've visited?"

- "What's the last big adventure you've gone on?"

## Other Fun Questions

- "What kind of music do you love to dance to?"

- "What's something that I wouldn't guess about you?"

- "What's your favorite food?"

- "What's your favorite meal to cook?"

- "What's your favorite dessert?"

## Recap of Flirty Questions to Use

- "What do you find sexy in a guy?"

- "What kinds of things make you laugh the hardest?"

- "What's the worst first date you've ever been on?"

Obviously, you don't want to ask these questions all in a row—instead, use a few of them throughout the conversation to get to know her. With each question, actively listen and relate back with your own experiences and thoughts. Then follow up and get to the next layer.

**For example,** if she tells you what she wanted to be when she grew up (but ended up going in a different direction), you can ask what made her decide to move away from that—and there may even be some room to give her a little motivation to try it again. What's more, many of these questions will give you fodder to tease and flirt with her.

## Hometown Teasing

**You:** "What was your favorite thing about growing up in (her hometown)?" Her: (mentions loving the local music scene) You: "You were totally the rebel girl sneaking out to concerts as a teenager, weren't you?"

## Food Future Projection

**You:** "What's your favorite meal to cook?" Her: (talks about her favorite dish to cook) You: "Sounds delicious. All right—we'll have to have a cooking night then. You cook, I'll bring the wine, and we'll call it a perfect night in. Fair warning, though: I'm a tough critic in the kitchen."

## The Salsa Innuendo

**You:** "What kind of music do you love to dance to?" Her: (talks about loving salsa dancing) You: "Ah, so you've got some rhythm—that's important for a lot of things. I like that. I've got a few salsa dancing moves under my belt, too. We'll have to hit the dance floor one day!"

Keep in mind that on first dates, you'll be diving deep, weaving in flirting, and gently guiding things forward. Everything she tells you is a potential new conversation thread that you can use to flirt or get to know her on a deeper level. Remember to use some of the flirting techniques uncovered in this book as well.

## Use Physical Flirting Throughout

So far, we've examined the importance of physical touch and flirting, but let's take a quick look into how to do it specifically on first dates.

**First, why is physical touch important on the first date? It accomplishes a number of things:**

- **Breaks the Touch Barrier:** Early on, casual touches (like greeting her with a hug or playfully touching her arm during a joke) can break the initial barrier, making more intimate touches (like putting your hand on her leg or going for a quick kiss) feel more natural later.

- **Creates Comfort and Connection:** Physical touch creates a sense of closeness and shared intimacy.

- **Tests her investment:** Does she freeze up with your touch, act neutral, or melt into it? Her reaction tells you a lot about her current interest and investment levels, and it also lets you know how ready she is to escalate things further.

- **Shows Dominance:** A guy who isn't afraid to get physical and go for what he wants is much more attractive than the guy who overthinks every single move.

**Below are some ways that you can add physical touch into your dates:**

- **The Greeting:** Start with the quick, warm hug described earlier.

- **Light, Casual Touches:** Look for natural opportunities for touch at high points, like when you're both laughing.

  o **For example,** you can gently nudge her arm when teasing her or give her a high five (and see if she clasps your fingers).

- **Guiding Gestures:** If you're moving to a new location or working your way through a crowd, guide her with a light touch on the small of her back.

- **Shared Activities:** You can do things that naturally require touch, like jokingly testing her biceps strength, comparing hand sizes (just make sure that you have bigger hands than her), or gently grasping her hand and asking about her rings or other jewelry.

- **Subtle Escalation:** If she's responding positively to light contact, you might touch her hair while complimenting it or briefly place your hand on her knee during a deeper part of the conversation. Always be mindful of her reactions, and back off if she seems stiff or freezes up.

- **The Quick Kiss:** Give her the quick three-to-five-second kiss mentioned earlier, and be the first one to pull back.

## Key Takeaways

- **Recognize Her Interest:** Her presence on the date is already a sign of interest. She's intrigued and so the stage is set for you—not to prove your worth but to build on the existing attraction.

- **Cost-Effective Dates Matter:** Keep dates affordable—think coffee and a walk or drinks at a bar. There's no need to overdo it by insisting on an expensive dinner.

- **Flirting Helps Enhance the Connection:** Use teasing, playful banter, as well as deeper conversation topics to create a more in-depth exchange. Mix genuine curiosity with light-hearted teasing to keep the mood fun.

- **Leading the Interaction:** Guide the date from the start—from the greeting hug to choosing where to sit. This sets the tone and makes you come across confidently.

- **Be Aware of Her Responses:** Pay attention to her reactions to both your conversation and physical advances. Her comfort levels will let you know the right time to escalate things.

# Flirting With a Group

The idea of flirting with or even approaching a group of girls may seem daunting, especially if you get anxious about talking to a single girl. But with the right approach and mindset, it's easier than you might think.

Let's get into how to meet women in groups and weave flirting in along the way.

## Reframing the Group Approach

Let's get something straight: Walking up to a group of girls might feel like you're stepping into the lion's den, but here's a hot take—not only is it completely doable but it's often easier than talking to a girl solo, and it can even be more fun. Here's why:

### It Provides a Conversational Buffer

Think about it. In a one-on-one situation, the spotlight's all on you to keep the conversation flowing. But in a group? You've got multiple women bouncing off each other, making the interaction more dynamic and less about you having to carry the whole show. It's like having a safety net—the girls can talk among themselves, which gives you room to observe, chip in, and steer the conversation forward.

### Showcase Your Social Savvy

Sure, it can be a bit of a hurdle to get the whole group to warm up to you, but once they do, you're golden. Winning over the group often means that you've passed a collective test of coolness—it's like getting multiple stamps of approval from her friends, which makes narrowing in on the girl you're into a smoother ride.

### You've Got a Head Start

Walking up to a group of girls by yourself might seem like a mission for two, but here's where the solo approach has its perks. It shows confidence and self-assuredness. Strolling in there without backup sends a message that you're confident in your own skin, and that's a major turn on. Plus, once you hold things down for a few minutes and win the group over, it's easy for your friends to join in and play good wingmen.

# Understanding Group Dynamics

There are a few different group dynamics you'll come into contact with, and you'll want to navigate each of them a little differently. Let's take a look at the main ones:

### The Duo

This is actually slightly more challenging than a group of three or more girls. It can feel like you're interrupting a private party, making it harder to isolate the girl you like. After all, it's not the most savvy move to take her away and leave her friend all alone.

The move here is to give them *both* the spotlight. If you're in a nightlife setting, you can approach with something simple, like, "You girls look like fun. How's your night going?" Make sure that you bring a smile and positive energy when you do this.

If it's during the day, the easiest thing is to either go with something situational or ask for directions, getting them both involved in the conversation.

**For example:** "Hey, I know this is a little random, but y'all seem hip and like you know the area. I'm looking for a good coffee place here— do you have any recommendations?"

Keep in mind that in two-girl groups, you've basically got to do everything together. If you're getting a drink, checking out a different area of the venue, or going on a mini adventure, you've got to bring the friend along—at least until she gets picked off by another opportunistic guy. And if she's attractive, this often does happen.

## The Larger Group

With three or more girls, the dynamic shifts. Isolating your girl becomes a greater possibility, as her friends will still have company with each other. In nightlife venues, you can use the same "You guys look like fun" line, as it works well.

If it's during the day, you can ask for directions and then interlude by saying that they seem like fun, and then keep the conversation going. Or, if you're feeling courageous, you can simply go direct and say, "Excuse me, ladies—I know this is random, but I saw your friend walking here and I thought that she was the most beautiful girl I've seen all day, and so I had to meet her quickly." Then turn to the friend, introduce yourself, and turn back to the group and ask, "What are you ladies up to?" This might seem a little far-fetched, but if done smoothly, it can work like a charm.

Check out a clip of me doing this with a group of girls on the Venice Beach boardwalk here: https://bit.ly/group-approaching.

## The Mixed Group

If you're beginner level, so to speak, I'd recommend sticking with girl-only groups until you get some experience under your belt. Once you do, you'll start recognizing more opportunities and become more comfortable stepping into them.

Also, you just might see a beautiful girl you want to talk to but she's flanked by a guy or two in her group. Most guys would shy away from this, but now you'll have the skills and awareness to handle it.

The best way to approach the mixed group is by starting with the guys. You can start by dropping a compliment—something as simple as saying you like their shirt, shoes, or style, and giving them a "cheers." Once you chop it up with the guys for a couple of minutes, you can ask how they know the rest of the group. This gives you an understanding of the group dynamic, as well as which girls are off limits (if any).

Once they introduce you to the rest of the group, you can cautiously work your way in. Just don't completely ignore the guys. Keep them involved in the conversation, at least for the early stages, and this will help you earn their trust.

Keep in mind that not all mixed groups will be open to mingling with you. Some guys will see what you're doing immediately and completely shut you down. The better your vibe, the more open groups will generally be to meeting you.

# Flirting During Group Interactions

Here's a key thing to remember in group interactions: If the friends don't like or trust you, it'll be hard to make anything happen—even if your girl is into you. You need to keep the group involved and engaged early on so as to not make it seem like you're only interested in their friend and don't care about them at all.

## How to Flirt Like a Pro in Group Settings

Flirting with a group is a bit like you're the conductor of an orchestra— you've got to harmonize different elements and personalities to create a symphony. And it all starts from the very beginning.

### Engage The Whole Group Initially

- **Strategy:** Start by engaging the entire group to avoid coming off as rude or too direct. This establishes you as friendly and socially savvy. You'd likely be surprised how many guys single out the girl they like from the start and ignore everyone else. Bad move.

- **Example:** Walk up to the group and, with a playful tone, say, "Alright, I need a quick opinion here. Who's the best at giving advice on (a light topic like music, movies, etc.)?"

### Playfully Involve the Group in Flirting

- **Strategy:** Use the group's dynamics to your advantage. Make light-hearted assumptions or playful guesses that include everyone.

- **Example:** Pointing to the girl you're interested in, turn to her friends and playfully say, "She's a Scorpio, isn't she?" or "She's the troublemaker of the group, isn't she?"

**Discover the Relationship Dynamics**

- **Strategy:** Find out how the group knows each other, which gives you valuable info (are they best friends, family, coworkers?). They may act differently according to the group dynamic and,

    o **For example,** be more reserved around other coworkers (but not always!). Plus, you can tease them about the relationship dynamic.

- **Example 1:**

    o You: "So how do you guys all know each other?"

    o Them: (explains that they're co-workers)

    o You: "Okay, so who's the one who's always stealing all the lunches from the fridge?"

- **Example 2:**

    o If it seems like they're newer acquaintances, you can tease them with something fun like, "You all have this 'we just met but we're already friends' energy. Tinder group date?"

Along with these examples, you also have the "best friend test," in which you simply ask, "You guys are best friends, aren't you?" They'll usually say, "Yes! How'd you know?!" and you can run with it from there.

While doing all of this, you can essentially treat the group as one big flirting interaction. Make eye contact with all of them, lightly flirt, and ask some light connecting questions. Then you can bring it back to the girl you like when it's possible. This helps you win over the group and get their approval, and it also gives you the best chance to win over the one you like.

# Getting Alone Time with Your Girl

I'll be real with you: It's pretty fun once you really get a handle on managing group flirting dynamics. It kind of makes you feel unstoppable and gives you the confidence of knowing that no group or interaction is off limits.

But you're not here because it's fun to handle group dynamics—you're here because you want to get the girl! And to do that, you've got to find a way to isolate her away from the group and get some alone time.

## Transitioning from the Group to One on One

- **Strategy:** After about five to ten minutes of group engagement, it's time to focus on your girl. The key here is to do it in a way that feels natural and unforced.

- **Approach:** Casually suggest an activity that naturally requires fewer people. For instance, say to her, "Hey, have you tried the spicy margarita at the bar here? Let's go grab one—I've heard good things about it." This approach is non-threatening and offers a good reason to separate from the group, even just momentarily. You can even ask permission from the group if you want to, and playfully say something like, "You guys cool if I steal your friend to grab a drink for a few minutes? I promise I'll bring her back safe." If you've managed the group dynamics as suggested above, they should be totally cool with it.

**Handling a Duo:** When It's Her & Her Friend

- **Strategy:** In case you're dealing with two girls, you don't want to leave one of them hanging—that's a fast track to making a bad impression.

- **Approach:** Engage both of them in the transition. For instance, "You guys must try the mojitos here. Let's go—I'll show you." This keeps the vibe friendly and inclusive, and it also shows that you're considerate of her friend. Hopefully at some point, another guy approaches the friend. If not, you can entertain them both, and if they're feeling adventurous, you may have an opportunity to go somewhere in private with them both (although this is a little more of an advanced strategy). If you're not at that level yet, you can always work out the logistics, make sure that the friend can get home safe at the end of the night, and then you'll have some alone time with your girl.

## The Back-and-Forth Dance: Building Investment

- **Tactic:** Once you've isolated her, it's not necessarily about staying away from the group for the rest of the night. Instead, you can use the opportunity to deepen your connection and then rejoin the group. This shows that you're social and respectful of her time with friends.

- **Execution:** After a bit of one-on-one time, suggest rejoining her friends. "Let's head back to your group—I don't want them thinking that I've kidnapped you." This balance between private and group interaction helps you build trust and exhibit your social savviness. You can have a bit of back-and-forth like this throughout the night, isolating and then rejoining the group.

## Sealing the Deal

- **Final Move:** As the night progresses and you feel a strong connection, you can consider taking things to the next level.

- **Suggestion:** If things are going well and she's following your lead, you might say, "I know this great spot nearby with an incredible view. Let's get out of here and check it out." It's important to read her cues—her level of comfort with you tells you everything you need to know.

## Final Pointers for Groups

- **Respect the Friends:** Always acknowledge and respect her friends. Winning them over is just as important as winning your girl. If her friend goes full "Karen" on you because of your sloppy approach, you're in for a rough time.

- **Maintain a Connection with the Group:** Keep touching base with the group throughout the night. It shows that you're considerate and not just there for a quick pick up.

- **Identify the "Leader" of the Group:** The "alpha" of the group will have the biggest influence over the others. If you get *her* on your side, everything else becomes easier.

- **Plan Your Exit (If needed):** If the vibe isn't right or if the group isn't receptive to your presence, be ready to gracefully exit the conversation. A simple "Great chatting with you—enjoy your evening!" is all you need.

- **Smooth Transitions:** Watch for opportunities in the conversation where you can naturally shift your focus to the girl you like.

  o **For example**, if she mentions something that you're also interested in, use that as a segue.

## Key Takeaways

- **Embrace the Group Dynamic:** Think approaching a group is scary? Flip the script and make it an opportunity. Chatting with a group takes the pressure off of you to keep the conversation going all by yourself.

- **Understand Different Group Setups:** Each group dynamic needs its own playbook. Duos are a balancing act, so you need to include both of them to avoid leaving anyone out. Larger groups? You've got more wiggle room to focus on and isolate the girl you're interested in, but make sure that you're engaging the whole group first. Mixed company? Make friends with the guys to build trust.

- **Flirting Tactics for Groups:** Use playful banter or make light-hearted guesses about the group or your girl. This will make everyone's night more fun, and the group will be glad they met you.

- **Smooth Moves for One-on-One Time:** Got the group's approval? Time for some alone time with your girl. Suggest a side adventure—maybe a drink or a dance. Keep it laid back and casual, like it's just another fun twist in the night.

- **Sealing the Deal:** As the night goes on, suggest a change of scenery if you and your girl are vibing. It could be a quiet corner in the venue or a different spot altogether. The key? Just make sure that she's invested and following your lead before going in for the ask.

# Flirting Over Text & Dating Apps

Earlier in this book, we examined how women flirt over text messages, which showed you how to identify if a girl is interested and receptive.

But many guys struggle when it comes to texting. And after working with thousands of clients through dating coaching, I've seen *a lot* of guys make easily preventable texting errors that end up costing them dates.

This chapter will give you a great foundation with which to text women the right way so that you can stop missing out on opportunities.

## The 5 Texting Principles

### 1. Use Her Name

It's simple psychology—hearing (or reading) her name triggers a unique reaction in her brain, creating a sense of familiarity and comfort. This instantly personalizes your conversation and makes her feel like she's not just another contact in your phone. Kick off a new text thread by using her name, something along the lines of, "Hey Emily, it's (your name). I'm still looking for that perfect avocado."

### 2. Sound Smart but Casual

Well-written texts signal that you're intelligent and mature, while sloppy texts signal the opposite and can sometimes be a dealbreaker. You definitely want to avoid grammar mistakes and awkward formatting. That said, being too formal can be a buzzkill. You're not penning a college essay here.

The happy medium is smart but casual, like you're chatting with a friend you respect. No spelling mistakes, correct grammar and formatting, but not overly formal.

**For example:**

**Too formal:** "Hello (her name), let's go for a drink date this week. Are you going to be available on Tuesday or Thursday?"

**Just right:** "Hey (her name), let's grab drinks this week. You free Tuesday or Thursday?"

## 3. Match Her Response Time (To a Point)

If she takes hours to respond, and then once she does you text back within two minutes, you're going to seem a bit needy. Instead, match the tempo—if she takes 30 minutes to respond, then you should take anywhere from 20 to 40 minutes. This subtly communicates that you've got a life beyond your phone screen. But this doesn't mean that you should play games; if she's responsive and quick, feel free to keep the pace. Just avoid instant replies every time, as it can come off as you being too available.

But if she takes a day or two to respond, you won't be able to mirror that—it'll make for a pretty long and drawn-out conversation. Instead, in this case, respond a bit faster (maybe 30 minutes later) and keep it strictly logistical. Try to set up that date! Forget about small talk and building rapport at this point.

## 4. Less is More

You're not Will Shakespeare trying to write a love letter here—you don't need to engage in long, in-depth text conversations. The longer your texts, the harder it is to transition into an in-person meet up, and the more likely you are to be the "pen pal" stuck in the friendzone.

You should aim to go for the meet-up or date after you each send anywhere between four to seven texts. Any longer than that and you risk killing the tension and losing the girl. Also, avoid double and triple texting. If she doesn't respond for a bit, let it sit and give her a chance. Panicking and sending multiple texts will generally make you come off as needy.

## 5. Every Text Has a Purpose

Each you send should be, in some way, moving you closer to the next hangout. You don't need to get "too cute" and weave in all these intricate bits of flirting or ask her the perfect question. None of that is going to help and, in a lot of cases, can lead to over-validating the girl to the point where she's not that excited to hang with you anymore.

Instead, aim to push the conversation toward a meet-up. Cut out the filler questions and focus on building up to that date. Before sending a message, ask yourself, "Is this text moving me closer to my goal?" If it's not clearly serving a purpose, don't send it.

**For example**, before the first date, you wouldn't want to text her, "Anyway, what places have you always wanted to travel to?" That's a question you'd ask on the first date. But if she texts *you* a question like that, you could say, "More fun to talk about that over drinks (wink emoji). How's tomorrow or Thursday sound?"

# Flirting Over Text Before the First Date

At this point, you don't have much buy-in or investment from the girl yet, especially if you've only had a quick interaction with her. That said, the stronger your communication and flirting fundamentals are, the more excited she'll be to meet you. You'll have a little wiggle room to make some mistakes. But either way, it's better to have a clean, easy texting plan you can use for light banter, followed by asking her out.

Once you get her number and while you're still with her, text her your name and location. If you're meeting her at the grocery store, you'd just text, "Mark - supermarket" and make sure that it went through on her phone. Then tell her it was good to meet her and that you'll text her later on. This sets expectations and keeps things simple.

If you're in a nightlife setting and you exchange Instagrams, you can take a quick smiling selfie of the two of you and have that be the first direct message. And if you're feeling confident, you can tell her to kiss you on the cheek in the picture.

And from there, let it sit for a bit—you'll want to wait before sending her the second text. If you met her during the day (say, before 5 pm), you can text her later that evening after 8 pm. If you met her at night (any time after 5 pm), you can text her the next day around noon.

That second text will be the "callback humor" text. This jogs her memory of who you are and brings back the positive emotions she felt when she met you. This is a lot better than the "Hey, how are you?" or "Did you have fun last night?" texts that most guys send. It'll help you stand out—*and* get a response.

## Callback Humor in Action

Below are some examples to build off of. Keep in mind that you can use a subtle laughing emoji at the end of the texts to spice them up a bit. But remember not to overdo it—don't use emojis in every text or multiple emojis at a time.

**Premise:** You talked to her about how much the two of you like Mexican food.

**Callback Text:** "Hey (her name), fun meeting you last night. I've been craving breakfast tacos ever since we talked."

**Premise:** You asked for directions to Starbucks, then told her that you thought she was cute.

**Callback Text:** "Hey (her name), honestly never found Starbucks yesterday. Still searching for my coffee."

**Premise:** You joked about travel destinations.

**Callback Text:** "Hey (her name), caught myself planning our imaginary trip to Rome over breakfast. Hope you're ready for some gelato and history! "

**Premise:** You met at the gym and she gave you some leg workout tips.

**Callback Text:** "Hey (her name), my legs are still killing me from that workout. Thanks for that! "

## Bridging the Conversation

Once you've dropped some callback humor and she's responded well, you've got to keep the conversation moving forward. This is your "bridge."

To bridge the conversation, simply add value and then ask about her day.

**For example:**

**Callback Text:** "Hey (her name), caught myself planning our imaginary trip to Rome over breakfast. Hope you're ready for some gelato and history! "

**Her Response**: "Haha, I'm already fantasizing about pasta!"

**Your Bridge:** "Get that appetite going, ha. Anyway, I just got a great workout in (this adds value). How's your Thursday going?"

You basically insert some quick, interesting info about your day (the value) and then ask about hers. This gives her something to work with. **Some other value phrases could be:**

- "Currently blasting (famous music artist) on the way to the gym."

- "Just hit the beach and got an early surf in."

- "Just crushed my last bit of work for the day."

- "Currently walking through downtown and taking in some sun."

Once she responds to that, there may be one more line of banter you can use, but it actually may not be needed depending on her response.

**If she seems interested, you can go right for the date from there:**

"Anyway, you seem like fun. Let's grab a drink this week. You free Tuesday or Thursday?"

Keep the following in mind: When you suggest a date, never call it a "date," as it can feel a bit too formal. Also, always give her two options for when to meet, and if neither of those work for her, she can suggest another day. When picking these days, aim to set the date up within two to four days, as the "flake rate" can skyrocket if it's any longer than that.

Then, once you set up the date, make sure to confirm it the day before. This can just be a simple text like, "Hey (her name), we still all good for tomorrow at 7 pm at McCarthy's Pub?"

Once she confirms, you can then respond the day of and say, "Sounds good, see you there." This adds a little extra confirmation without needing to ask.

Confirming makes the date real in her mind, and so she'll be less likely to flake.

## Flirting Over Text After the First Date

Once you've had a solid first date, you'll have more buy-in from here. But bear in mind that you can still screw things up with the wrong texts!

**Here are a few mistakes you'll want to avoid:**

- **Immediately Trying to Schedule the Next Date:** Going in for the second date right away makes you come off as way too eager and desperate. It's much better to give it a few days to breathe before asking again. You can still text with some callback humor the next day, but then let it sit before re-initiating the conversation and going for the hangout. So, if you sent callback humor on Tuesday and got a good response, wait until Thursday or Friday to reach out again (with the same format you used before the first date—bridge, banter, then ask) to plan the next one.

- **Becoming Her Texting Buddy:** Guys will have a great meet-up with a girl and then try to text her all the time afterwards. You guys *aren't* on that level yet. Doing this will just over validate her and get her less excited about the second date. Remember Dex's principle: "Be gone," as it definitely applies here.

- **Don't Panic:** If you don't get a response right away, stay calm and go on with your day. At this point, you've done your job, and the rest is on her.

A great way to reach out again if you haven't texted her in a few days is to send a quick ten-second video message. The key here is to record it with upbeat energy and tonality—it's a really solid way to stand out.

**Check out this example of me recording a video message, and just follow the format:** https://bit.ly/dave-video-text.

## Flirting Over Text Three or More Dates In

At this point you've got a lot of buy in from her (as long as you've been running the dates well and using the flirting techniques we've covered).

You really don't need to do anything special here. You can follow the same format: callback humor after the date, some banter in between, and then planning the next hang out. There may be a little more banter in between as you hang out with her more and build rapport and comfort. The hangouts may start to happen gradually more frequently as well—and all of that is fine.

Ideally, after three to five dates and you've gotten intimate, she should be texting you a little more eagerly and coming up with date ideas herself. This isn't always the case, though—some girls text more than others, so don't sweat it either way.

# How to Flirt in Online Dating

Flirting online is very similar to flirting over text, and many of the girls you text may be from online dating interactions anyway, so there's a lot of overlap.

The main difference is that you've got to get her engaged at the start before she's met you.

If you have a solid dating profile with optimized photos, this becomes far, far easier. It's even easier if you link your dating profile to your (optimized) Instagram account.

Your photos and profile will do much of the work for you. Great flirting won't make up for terrible photos, and great photos will give you more wiggle room to screw things up on the flirting. That's why, before anything else with online dating, you need to make sure that your photos, bio, and prompts are on point, or else this is all for naught.

**If you want to understand what high-quality dating photos look like, check out the IG for Beast Photos:** https://www.instagram.com/beastphotos_official/. You can use this for posing, background, and style inspiration as well.

Aside from that, you might be wondering, "Once I match with a girl, then what do I do?" I could give you some go-to openers as examples, but that wouldn't make sense here. Every guy would just copy and paste them in and they'd become overused. And I don't want you getting called out for using some line that the last ten guys she's talked to have used! Instead, I'm going to give you the principles behind great initial messages so that it'll be easy for you to craft them in your own style.

## The Anatomy of a Winning First Message

- **Easy to Respond To:** Don't try to be "too clever." This makes it harder for the girl to respond, because she'll feel as if she needs to come up with something clever, too. The easier your message is to respond to, the more likely it'll get a response, and that's the whole point—to get the conversation going.

- **Creates a Fun and Flirty Vibe:** You want to avoid the "friend zone" from the start, so your first message should create a flirty dynamic that'll help you get her attracted.

- **Stands Out (At Least a Little):** If you send the same types of messages that every other guy sends, you'll get the same types of responses (usually nothing). You don't need to do anything crazy—but just don't be so predictable. Always avoid "Hey, how are you?" messages.

One of the easiest things you can do is point out something from her profile or bio, and then use that as the initial message. This ensures that it's unique.

Once you've sent a solid first message and get a response, you can have a few lines of banter, similar to what we covered in the texting section above. Then, after four or five messages, ask if she wants to hang out.

Once she says yes, grab her number or Instagram and move things off the app.

## Key Takeaways

- **Follow the Texting Principles:** Use her name, sound smart but casual, match her response time, and text with a purpose.

- **Open with Callback Humor:** This helps jog her memory and brings up the positive emotions she associated with your initial conversation.

- **Use Texting Bridges:** After your callback humor text, shift to simple rapport-building questions, like asking about her day. This keeps the conversation moving forward and sets you up for suggesting a meet-up.

- **Confirm the Date the Day Before:** This helps you avoid getting stood up and flaked on, and it also shows respect for your time.

- **Texting After the Date:** The next day, send callback humor established during the date, but don't go for the second date right away. Let it sit for a few days, then re-initiate. Once she responds, you can start planning out the next date.

- **Online Dating Flirting:** Your first message should be fun, flirty, and somewhat unique. The easiest way to do this is to use something on her profile to start the conversation. Then, push for the date within the first four to six messages.

# Part 4

# How to Be a Natural at Flirting

# The 10 Raw Skills That Make You Better at Flirting

There may have been moments throughout this book when you've thought, "That's awesome advice...but I'm not good at that!" or "That doesn't come naturally to me!"

But here's the thing: The beautiful part of flirting is that it's a skill. And like any skill, it can be learned, and there are certain things that you can do to accelerate that learning process.

This is where the raw skills of flirting come into play. The more you improve on each of these skills, the better you'll be at flirting and communication. And thankfully, these skills are all actually *fun* to learn.

I'll start by laying out the skills and explaining them. Then, in the next chapter, we'll examine how exactly you can develop each of these skills and truly become a natural at flirting.

## The 10 Flirting Raw Skills

## 1. Wittiness

When it comes to flirting, wittiness means that you can think quickly and come up with clever responses that add a spark to the conversation. It's about finding the fun, clever angle and using it to your advantage.

Wittiness keeps conversations lively and interesting, and it also makes your interactions memorable and engaging. It could be that innuendo you come up with on the spot that adds a little spice, or maybe that quick comeback when she tries to test you.

If you've got wittiness, everything else with flirting becomes easier.

One helpful technique to be more witty is to agree and exaggerate when she tests you.

**For example**, if she says, "You're too young for me," you could agree and exaggerate with something like, "Of course I am. I'll have to slow down a little so that you can keep up."

## 2. Reduced Self-Monitoring

But you can be witty in a platonic way, too, so that's not enough. You still need a little bit of an edge that turns your flirting from friendly to sexy. And if you constantly filter yourself, you won't have that.

That's where reduced self-monitoring comes in. This is the ability to express yourself freely and spontaneously without over analyzing or excessively censoring yourself. It's an essential skill that involves lowering the filter that checks and modifies your behavior and speech when you're talking to women.

High levels of self-monitoring can make your conversations seem rehearsed, scripted, or artificial, but good flirting thrives on spontaneity and authenticity.

And here's a trade secret for you: If I had to point to just one thing that made me great at flirting so quickly, it's this very skill.

I started by completely removing my filter, which I had some success with but wasn't exactly the right move—I'd sometimes cross the line a little too often and offend people. So I added it back in at a low level, and it honestly elevated my flirting to new heights.

Most guys have a very heavy filter. This causes them to be self-conscious and more calculating, and it doesn't allow the interaction to flow.

As you lower your filter, your conversations will flow more smoothly and you'll come off with just the right amount of "edge."

There are many guys out there who are concerned about "running out of things to say." What's ironic is that you may know exactly what to say in the moment but you convince yourself that it's a bad idea. Just start by saying that "thing" and see how it goes!

## 3. Sense of Humor

Having a sense of humor isn't just about making someone laugh—it's more about viewing the world through a playful lens and bringing a little flavor and joy into interactions.

It shows that you don't take yourself too seriously and that you're always up for a little fun.

The point here isn't to be the "class clown" or constantly add jokes to the conversations—that can make you seem a little too goofy. It's more about sprinkling in some well-timed humor at different points throughout the conversation.

# 4. Storytelling

The world is run by stories—after all, it's how we communicate. And the guys who are the best with women are *great* storytellers.

When you master the art of storytelling, you can captivate people and really bring them into your world. And this is especially powerful when communicating with women.

You're able to convey and make her feel emotions, showcase your communication skills, and engage her imagination.

Start by having a few go-to stories that you tell on dates and in your interactions. Really perfect those stories—tell them to yourself in the mirror, record them, and flesh them out so that it becomes second nature to tell them. The best stories showcase attractive qualities about yourself without outright bragging, all while keeping the woman engaged and interested.

# 5. Presence

This is about more than just being physically there—it's also about being mentally and emotionally tuned in.

When you're present, you can pick up on her social cues and guide the conversation in the right direction, and you're not overthinking or overanalyzing. You just let it flow.

An average guy might talk to a girl and think, "I wonder if she likes me" or "I don't want to say the wrong thing!", but a present guy isn't concerned with that. He enjoys the moment, the beauty of the woman, and the interaction.

This presence builds trust and helps create intimacy. She can tell that you're fully tuned in, and she can relax a bit more in your presence.

# 6. Empathy

Great flirting requires a certain level of comfort. She's got to feel okay being a little vulnerable with you, and that's where empathy comes into play.

Basically, empathy is the ability to understand and share her feelings, and it's a key element in coming across with more warmth.

This allows you to tune into her emotional cues more. Is she hesitant, enthusiastic, amused, or intrigued? You can pick up on these cues and direct the conversation in the right way.

# 7. Self-Amusement

This skill comes back to having a playful approach to life and not taking yourself too seriously. Self-amusement boils down to being able to find joy and humor in your interactions—not solely for the entertainment of the girl but also for your own genuine enjoyment.

You're not "performing" or trying to impress. You're your own source of fun, and she's invited to join in. The beauty of this is that it takes the pressure off. She can choose to join in on the fun, but if not, it's her loss.

# 8. Self-Acceptance

If you're overloaded with insecurities, you'll have a hard time flirting well. You'll overthink everything, which will slow you down and make you seem stiff. You'll also have a tendency to mask your true self, and that'll hinder any connection that you're trying to build.

That's why self-acceptance is key. When you're genuinely okay with who you are, you can express yourself authentically without fear. You can make that joke, talk about your hobbies, and share your real perspective. And none of it will be a facade.

Plus, you'll be more resilient to rejection. If she doesn't like your flirting style or a certain tease that you make, it won't make you doubt yourself or your worth. You *know* that you're enough—despite what any woman may think. Self-acceptance gives you freedom and allows you to communicate in a way that other guys can't.

# 9. Leading

**Most guys go into their interactions with literally zero idea of how they'll move things forward:**

"It seems like she likes me. What do I do now?" "She's giving me a test. What does it mean?" They have no guiding structure or plan for what's going to happen when things go well—or when they go poorly. They just sort of do things and hope for the best, and this is a losing strategy.

When you're flirting, you should be gently guiding and leading the interaction somewhere. This could be toward getting her to invest more in the interaction, spiking her emotions, or even leading toward a physical location, like another venue or somewhere more private.

When you're leading, you've got some sort of logistics or goal in the back of your mind. You're still in the moment while flirting, but you know where you want things to end up.

# 10. Spontaneity

This is all about being creative and responsive in the moment, and even a little impulsive at times. It adds an element of surprise and keeps the women you're talking to on their toes. It makes you unpredictable, helping you to break their patterns and really engage with you.

Spontaneity could show up as a spur-of-the-moment, adventurous idea that you bring up, or as a quick joke or innuendo that you make.

Here's an example. Back in my early twenties, I took a trip to San Diego, and I found myself on a date with a beautiful girl on my last night there. But logistically, there was nowhere we could go to get intimate—her place was unavailable and I was staying at a friend's house.

So with nothing to lose, **I made a spontaneous move:** "Look, I think you're cool and I'm super attracted to you. I'm enjoying my time with you, but you know I'm going to be leaving tomorrow. So is it okay if I make a proposition that might seem a little crazy?"

"What is it?!" she laughed.

"What if we drive to the beach, lay out a blanket, and (get intimate) under the stars?" I asked, grinning. I figured I might as well shoot my shot.

"Oh my God!" she said, taken aback for a moment. "I've never done anything like that before, and we just met…"

"Yeah, I know it's a little crazy. I'm cool either way. If you want to continue the adventure, I'm up for that. And if not, it's been amazing hanging out," I said.

She paused for a second and laughed. And then:

"Well…I *do* have a sleeping bag in my car we could lay out…and there's this quiet beach we could drive to where nobody would bother us…"

"So…you want to make this adventure happen then?" I asked.

"You know what? Yes, let's do it!" she smiled.

Needless to say, that turned into a *very* memorable night.

Now, that's not a move that I'd typically recommend, and I'm guessing that it likely has a fairly low success rate. But sometimes the moment calls for a little spontaneity, and if you're willing to step up and go for it, you can have some amazing adventures.

It also illustrates just how much great flirting can change things. Had the flirting not been dialed in, there's no way that she would've been open to it. But because she felt that we were both on the same team and like I wasn't going to judge her, she was willing to do something out of the ordinary.

Spontaneity in your actions and words can help you give her unique experiences while making you memorable.

Now that we're at the end of this chapter, you might be thinking, "These are a lot of skills. How am I going to master all of these?" Thankfully, it's a lot simpler than you think, because many of these skills have overlap. There are a few quick daily and weekly activities that you can do to hone them in and become a natural at flirting. And that's exactly what we'll dive into in the next chapter.

## Key Takeaways

- **Raw Skills:** There are certain things that just make you better at flirting. Once you get these raw skills down, flirting and banter will come naturally.

- **Develop Your Wit:** Quick, clever responses add fun to your flirting and keep her guessing.

- **Reduce Your Self-Monitoring:** When you lower your internal filter, you can express yourself more freely and authentically, allowing you to take more risks in your conversations.

- **Build Your Sense of Humor:** This allows you to add more fun and playfulness to your interactions without coming across as goofy.

- **Storytelling:** Have a few stories under your belt that you can bring out in your conversations.

- **Presence and Empathy:** These qualities help you to better pick up on social and emotional cues, encourage her to feel safe around you, and make the interaction more memorable.

- **Self-Amusement and Acceptance:** These help you reduce your fear of rejection, enjoy interactions more, and not be negatively impacted if a conversation doesn't go your way.

- **Leading:** This skill allows you to guide things forward so that you're flirting with a purpose.

- **Spontaneity:** Being spontaneous with your words and actions adds excitement. It makes your interactions more compelling and opens the door to fun, shared adventures with women.

# How to Build the Raw Flirting Skills and Become a Natural with Women

Now that you know the key raw flirting skills, you're likely wondering how to actually build them.

As I promised in the last chapter, the skills are actually pretty fun and easy to learn. And they won't just help you with flirting—they'll also help you become a better communicator, more confident, and more decisive.

To be fair, you may look at some of these suggestions and wonder, "What the heck is this guy talking about?" or "That seems weird!"

But hey—all I ask is for you to keep an open mind. I've done all of these activities myself, taught them to thousands of men, and seen them make a huge impact firsthand.

## Activities to Build Your Flirting Skills

### Stand-Up Comedy & Improv

My father, John Perrotta, happens to be a stand-up comic. He's opened for some of the biggest comics in the game, from Bill Burr to Dane Cook and many more. If you've been to any comedy shows in the New England area, you may have heard of him. He's known as the "Italian Don Rickles."

Don Rickles is a legendary comedian widely known for his sharp wit and crowd work. And just like Don, my father *loves* to work the crowd.

146

He'll go up and down the room and ask people what they do for work, how they know each other, and deliver quick quips along the way—all while bringing plenty of energy and basically having the presence of a mob boss. Ironically, he's also known as "The Godfather" of Rhode Island comedy.

The point of all this isn't to promote my dad (though you might want to see one of his shows if you find yourself in New England!). It's to say that ever since I can remember, I was attending my dad's stand-up comedy shows and watching him do crowd work, as well as bearing witness to all the other comics he brought up along the way.

And it had a *big* impact on the way I communicate myself, even if I didn't realize it at the time. I'd pick up on the way he teased the crowd and would come to tease women in a similar way as I got older. I adopted his quick wit and wordplay as well, and I learned to weave them into fun innuendos and use wit to pass any woman's tests.

Looking back, this was a big part of the reason that I was able to "get good" with women faster than most. It was because I'd already built a lot of the raw skills of flirting by accident. (Thanks, Dad!)

And that's why I always recommend to guys that they watch stand-up comedy, especially comedians that are great at one-liners and crowdwork. If you watch five to ten minutes a day of these guys for a few months, it'll start to seep into the way you talk and interact with people in the best way possible.

**Here's a few excellent comedians for you to check out:**

- **Mark Normand:** The king of witty banter. He's got a one-liner for everything and is great at finding humor in everyday situations.

- **Sam Morrill:** He's known for his sharp wit and interesting commentary on dating, relationships, and the absurdities of modern life.

- **Bill Burr:** This guy is a great storyteller and can turn basically any subject into comedy gold.

- **Steven Wright:** He's renowned for his deadpan delivery and offbeat humor, along with some awesome one-liners.

- **Mitch Hedberg:** His laid-back demeanor and quirky one-liners can inspire you to bring a relaxed, playful energy to your flirting.

- **Andrew Schulz:** He has a boulder, boundary-pushing kind of comedic style. He's also got some amazing back-and-forths when he does crowd work, which can help strengthen your wit.

And, of course, if you want to try your own hand at stand-up comedy, that can be even better! There's plenty of open-mic nights in most big cities. If you're feeling up for the challenge, write down a quick five, get up there, and try it out for yourself.

Aside from stand-up comedy, improv can also be incredibly helpful with your wit and communication skills.

Essentially, improv is a form of live performance in which you create scenes, dialogues, and characters spontaneously and without a script. It's really easy to get into, and you can find affordable improv classes in any sizable city. I actually took improv classes early on in my dating journey and it made a big impact. Also, the nice bonus is that the classes are typically mostly women, and so you might even meet your next date there.

The really great thing about improv is that it forces you to think on your feet, release your fear of judgment, and adapt quickly to whatever is thrown your way—all key aspects of being great at flirting.

**Raw Skills You'll Improve with Stand-Up Comedy & Improv:**

- Quick wit

- Sense of humor

- Storytelling

- Self-amusement

- Reduced self-monitoring

- Spontaneity

## Freestyle Rapping & Word Association

I know that this one might sound a little ridiculous, but humor me—I promise that you'll thank me later when you're flirting like a pro.

Picture this for a second. You walk on stage in front of thousands of people—the beat is bumping, the crowd is watching, and it's your turn to step up. You've got no script and no safety net—just your wit, your words, and your rhythm.

This is the exact situation I found myself in back in the fall of 2012. My friends had put on a Big Sean concert in Connecticut, and I was backstage helping with the set up. Big Sean was one of the biggest up and coming rappers at the time. I'd developed some rapping chops in college, and so it was cool to see the whole spectacle. And then, out of nowhere:

"Hey, bro—one of the opening acts just backed out. We need a few rappers to go up and freestyle for a few minutes," my friend told me.

"If you're asking me, I'm in," I replied. I had zero doubt that I could pull this off. Within 20 minutes, I was on stage with a few other rappers in front of thousands of Big Sean fans. I grabbed the mic, the beat dropped, and I let it flow.

"I do this with a passion…fire-breathing dragon. They said it was a dream, I said I'd make it happen," I rapped.

And just like that…a star was born. (I'm kidding, obviously.)

I nervously muttered my way through the rest of the freestyle and made it work, but it certainly wasn't anything special. The crowd wasn't exactly blown away. But the point remains:

Number one, whenever you have the chance to do something epic, take it. Even if you screw it up, you'll have a good story to tell. This includes going up and talking to that beautiful girl.

Number two, freestyle rap is something that every man should learn to do. Why? Well, what if I told you that the very skills you hone with freestyle rap can transform your everyday conversations, particularly in the realm of flirting and social interactions?

Funnily enough, this was something I realized early on as well, and it was another thing that helped me greatly accelerate my communication with women. I'd grown up listening to stand-up comedy and had spent years honing my craft at freestyle rap. And so a talent for wit came naturally.

And it's not just me. Let's look at the findings of a study titled "Neural Correlates of Lyrical Improvisation: An fMRI Study of Freestyle Rap," conducted by Siyuan Liu et al. and published in *Scientific Reports* in 2012.

**Study Overview:**

**Objective:** To examine the neural correlates of improvised, creative verbal expression (in this case, freestyle rap).

**Participants:** The study involved skilled freestyle rap artists who had substantial experience in improvisational performance.

**What They Found:**

**Altered Brain Activity:** The most striking finding was that freestyle rapping led to a unique pattern of brain activity. Specifically, increased activity in regions associated with emotion, language, motivation (such as the amygdala, prefrontal cortex, and language areas like Broca's area) and a decrease in regions linked with executive functions (like the dorsolateral prefrontal cortex), which are responsible for controlling behavior and decision making.

**"Flow" State:** The decreased activity in executive parts of the brain is particularly interesting. It suggests that when rappers are freestyling, they might be in a "flow" state, in which self-monitoring and deliberative thought processes are reduced, allowing for more spontaneous and fluid verbal generation. This is specifically interesting for you. The decrease in activity in executive regions of the brain could be likened to reducing the "filter" in everyday conversation, which allows for more natural, spontaneous interactions—as well as better flirting.

**Enhanced Language and Emotional Expressivity:** Increased activity in language and emotional regions of the brain indicates that freestyle rap enhances one's ability to access and use a rich vocabulary, as well as to express emotions more effectively. In flirting, this translates to being able to play with words more skillfully and convey feelings and attraction more compellingly.

**Quick Thinking and Adaptability:** The improvisational nature of freestyle rap trains the brain to think quickly and adapt. When flirting, this skill helps you to respond swiftly to conversational cues, keep up with the dynamic flow of the interaction, and even turn potentially awkward moments into opportunities for humor or deeper connection.

**What All This Means for You:**

Basically, you should add freestyle rap into your arsenal. Even just five minutes a day while driving to work or when you're hanging at home alone can make a big difference. Throw on an instrumental beat from YouTube and just let it flow. You can even use a word generator website or app to help you come up with topics. The more you do this, the less you'll run out of things to say and struggle to keep up with a woman's wit.

**Raw Skills You'll Improve with Freestyle Rapping & Word Association:**

- Quick wit

- Self-amusement

- Reduced self-monitoring

- Presence

- Spontaneity

- Storytelling

- Self-acceptance

## Dance Classes

Every man should have at least a few dances moves up his sleeve.

Bachata, salsa, and country dancing are all solid options. Reggaeton is also great to learn if you want to get a little spicy with it.

These are all easy to learn with some beginner's dance classes. And what's great about dance classes is, like improv, they usually have more women than men, and so you'll likely meet some potential partners there, too.

Now, I'll stress here that I'm *far* from a dance expert. I've got four or five salsa and bachata moves that I can break out, but that's been enough for me to use on dates and at dance clubs. And it's especially helpful if you've got a thing for Latin women.

The point isn't to be a dance expert, though—it's more about the benefits of what a little bit of dancing can do for you.

It requires complete and immersive focus—you've got to be fully present in the moment. Dancing also helps you to connect with a woman not just physically but also emotionally, and so you're able to get more in tune with reading her cues.

It makes you better at leading, too. It's always the man's job to lead on the dance floor, just as it's his job to lead the conversations and dates. Dancing teaches you how to lead with assertiveness and empathy.

And as an added bonus, you can use dancing as a way to move things back to your place or hers. You can say, "Let's get out of here. I'd love to show you some of those dance moves we talked about." Or, once you're back home, you can show her a few bachata moves, which makes the mood intimate and provides an excuse to get physical.

**Raw Skills You'll Improve with Dance Classes:**

- Reduced self-monitoring

- Presence

- Spontaneity

- Self-acceptance

- Leading

- Empathy

## Sitting in Silence

We live in a high-stimulation world. At any given moment, you can scroll on X, watch a TikTok video, listen to a podcast, swipe on a dating app—or even do them all at once!

With so many options at your fingertips, it's easy to never "shut things off" and to rarely have time to yourself.

That's the power of sitting in silence. This could be five or ten minutes a day in which you meditate or just focus on your breathing. There are plenty of apps like Calm and Headspace that can help you with this. Or you can just toss on some meditation or breathing music and relax.

Sitting in silence will help you become more present and get you comfortable with "just being," and this calm presence is key to effective flirting. It can also allow you to self-reflect, and the time spent away from your screen can help reduce anxiety. That way, you can become cool, calm, and collected during decisive moments of flirting.

A variation of this is simply going on meditative walks. Just walk through a nice area or park with some meditative music—you'll get some daily steps in, and you might also have some opportunities to approach cute girls along the way.

**Raw Skills You'll Improve with Sitting in Silence:**

- Presence

- Self-acceptance

- Empathy

## Reading Fiction & Non-Fiction

At first, you may not connect the act of reading with your ability to flirt, but there's actually quite a bit of overlap.

**For example**, reading fiction helps improve your emotional intelligence, as it develops greater empathy and understanding of human emotions. It also broadens your imagination, which can help you have more engaging and creative conversations. It can expand your worldview, too, and make you a more intriguing and knowledgeable conversationalist.

Plus, it'll enable you to craft just the right dig when she tells you that she loved reading Harry Potter when she was younger.

Non-fiction, on the other hand, helps you to self-improve, informs you on a wide range of topics, and helps add more depth and substance to your personality.

You can add a daily reading habit of ten to fifteen minutes into your routine, mixing in both fiction and non-fiction books. I recommend reading non-fiction in the morning, as it can give you some ideas to ponder and take action on throughout your day. Fiction is best at night, as it's not too dense and can even help you fall asleep.

**Raw Skills You'll Improve with Reading Fiction & Non-Fiction:**

- Quick wit

- Self-amusement

- Self-acceptance

- Storytelling

- Empathy

## Going for the Close

You need to get into the habit of leading things to the next step with women. This could mean inviting her to the next venue, inviting her home, or respectfully going for intimacy once you're in a private location like your place or hers.

When you've employed the flirting techniques we've uncovered in this book, you'll attract women and be able to do so quite quickly. And you may be surprised at just how often women will want to take the next step with you—as long as you have the courage to ask for it.

One thing to keep in mind is that attraction has a window, and so you've got to act quickly once you have it. If you wait too long and miss your chance, you probably won't get another.

**Raw Skills You'll Improve with Going for the Close:**

- Leading

- Self-acceptance

- Spontaneity

- Reduced self-monitoring

## Consistent Action

Being consistent with all these activities will help you become a master at flirting, **but you've also got to take consistent action in *all* aspects of dating:**

- Getting premium photos for your dating profile so that you get more matches and dates

- Optimizing your Instagram so that you can convert more women from online dating and in-person approaches into first dates

- Starting conversations with women you find attractive in your day-to-day life

- Reflecting on what you can improve upon with each approach, conversation, and rejection

- Not giving up or settling when things feel a little bit difficult

**Raw Skills You'll Improve with Consistent Action:**

- All skills!

## Key Takeaways

- **Leverage Stand-Up Comedy and Improv:** These can enhance many of your raw flirting skills like quick wit, sense of humor, and spontaneity.

- **Freestyle Rap for Quick Thinking:** It'll train you to think on your feet and reduce self-monitoring. Plus, it can help you to never run out of things to say.

- **Develop Your Rhythm with Dance Classes:** Dance forms like salsa, bachata, and country can boost your confidence and help improve your presence, leading, and empathy when you flirt.

- **Sit in Silence:** Enhancing your presence and focus by sitting in silence or meditative walking—these can reduce anxiety and help you to be "in the moment" when you flirt.

- **Read Fiction and Non-Fiction:** Reading expands your emotional intelligence, as well as boosts your creativity, empathy, and conversation skills. It also makes you a better storyteller.

- **Go for the Close:** Confidently lead interactions toward the next step. Whether you move to a new venue or escalate to intimacy, timely action is key before the window of attraction closes.

- **Take Consistent Action:** Take action on the activities here along with everything else you've learned in this book. Optimize your dating profile and IG, approach women in your day-to-day life, and learn from each interaction.

# Final Thoughts

There are certain things in life that, once we do them, change us and we're never the same again. We forever stretch the limitations of what we initially thought was possible—climbing a mountain, running a marathon, skydiving, and I'm sure that you can think of a few others.

Improving our interactions with women and flirting belong in that category, too. I often call it the "gateway drug" to success in life.

There are so many men who spend their entire lives working on adjacent things, thinking that this will fix their dating life. They work on their finances, physique, career, appearance, and so on, only to then realize that all those things won't get them the kind of woman they want. To do that, they need to attack their dating life head on—with all the fears and insecurities that come along with it—and actually develop the communication skills that their dream woman craves in a man.

And once they decide to do this with intention, incredible changes can happen. They're fully at the helm now, and with more control than they've ever had before.

There's something magical about being able to walk up to a beautiful woman, get a conversation going, and know that you have a relatively good chance of attracting her. And if you can do that, what other incredible things are you capable of?

For myself and many of my clients, once we gained that ability and realization, we began to want more and more out of life. The idea of settling—something that may have once appealed to us in certain ways—no longer seems fulfilling.

The only way forward is to approach life in a full state of attack mode. You want something? Act in spite of your excuses and go for it. Something doesn't go your way? Take responsibility, make the necessary changes, and keep moving forward. There is no final failure—and no stopping until success is achieved.

And if you take this approach seriously, you'll open a door that most men never even have the courage to approach. You step into a world in which your full potential is on the table.

And that's kind of the point, isn't it?

You've only got one shot at this life, so there's no need to hold back.

## Key Takeaways of the Book

The main takeaway within these pages is that flirting is a learnable skill. It's not some kind of a magic "secret sauce" that only a few men are blessed with.

Take what's in these pages and use it to develop your skills, and I promise that you'll exponentially improve your dating life.

I've emphasized what flirting is and how to see it from the woman's perspective. You've learned how to meet beautiful women in different environments, how to apply flirting techniques in different situations, and how to become a natural at flirting through building the right raw skills.

You're now equipped with everything you need to get out there and have amazing conversations with women—conversations that'll get them attracted and keep them coming back for more.

Use your newfound skills wisely—remember to always have genuinely good intentions when you interact with women. They'll feel the love, kindness, and warmth behind your words, and become comfortable relaxing and showing you their "secret side" that they so rarely expose to men.

And that, my friends, is a magical thing.

# Your Next Step

If you apply what you learn in this book, you can build an amazing dating life for yourself.

But some of you may want to fast-track your success. After all, going at it alone isn't easy, even if you have the right tools and knowledge.

That's why I teamed up with David De Las Morenas from How to Beast to create the Beast Dating Coaching Program.

Through this program, we work with you personally to help you meet & attract amazing women, and build healthy relationships.

It's a very hands-on experience, and perfect for someone who wants to take this part of their life seriously, and have lots of accountability and support along the way.

If you'd like to learn more, just click the link below or scan the QR code to apply.

**Beast-coaching.com**

# A Parting Gift

As a way of saying thank you, I'm offering my **"Instant Attraction Toolkit"** that includes three FREE downloads exclusive to my book readers.

**Here's what you'll get:**

1.  **"The First Date Playbook":** A cheat sheet for first date success, with conversation starters, key questions to ask, and tips on creating a memorable experience. That way, you can get her attracted and keep her coming back for more.

2.  **"Get a Girlfriend in 30 Days - Audio Guide":** The exact step-by-step audio guide to meeting, attracting, and dating your dream girl in 30 days or less.

3.  **"5 Texting Mistakes that Destroy Attraction - Audio Guide":** Discover the texting mistakes that turn her off, derail her attraction, and make you look needy. That way, you can smoothly flirt over text, get more dates, and stop losing out on dating opportunities with beautiful women.

**Download your bonuses here:**

**Go to <u>daveperrotta.com/attraction</u> or scan the QR code below:**

# About the Author

Dave Perrotta is a dating coach, best-selling author, and entrepreneur. He's lived in over twenty different countries, and helped hundreds of thousands of men level up their dating life and find their life partners. **You can see dating tips from him on his podcast where he uploads new episodes every week:**

**Dating Decoded (on Spotify):** https://spoti.fi/3U6df37

# Can You Do Me a Favor?

*Thanks for checking out my book.*

I'm confident you will master conversation, connect with women, and flirt like a Casanova if you follow what's written inside. But before you go, I have one small favor to ask...

**Would you take 60 seconds and write a quick blurb about this book on Amazon?**

**You can do by navigating to the URL below or scanning the QR code:**

https://mybook.to/how-to-flirt

Reviews are the best way for independent authors (like me) to get noticed, sell more books, and spread my message to as many people as possible. I also read every review and use the feedback to write future revisions – and future books, even.

Thank you – I really appreciate your support.

Made in United States
Orlando, FL
06 July 2025

62684265R00095